Linux for Develo

Unlocking the Potential of Open-Source Tools

Theodore Bennett

Welcome to "Linux for Developers: Unlocking the Potential of Open-Source Tools." In an increasingly digital world, open-source software has become a driving force behind technological innovation, and Linux stands tall as a powerful and versatile operating system at its core. This book is designed to empower developers like you to harness the immense potential of Linux and leverage its open-source tools to build robust, scalable, and efficient software solutions.

Linux, with its roots dating back to the early 1990s, has evolved into a thriving ecosystem of distributions, libraries, frameworks, and utilities, all supported by a vibrant community of developers and enthusiasts. Its flexibility, security, and scalability make it a preferred choice for developers across various domains, including web development, system administration, cloud computing, and more.

Whether you are a seasoned developer seeking to expand your skills or a newcomer embarking on your coding journey, this book will serve as your comprehensive guide to Linux and its open-source tools. We will explore the fundamentals of Linux, delve into practical techniques for utilizing the command line, delve into shell scripting and automation, explore package management, and dive into version control with Git.

From there, we will journey into the realms of developing with Linux tools, uncovering the power of integrated development environments (IDEs), text editors, and debugging tools. We will then venture into the world of web development, where we will set up web servers, work with databases, and explore various programming languages and frameworks.

Containerization has revolutionized software development and deployment, and we will guide you through the popular Docker platform, allowing you to encapsulate your applications and streamline their deployment across environments. Networking, system administration, and security are essential aspects of any developer's skill set, and we will equip you with the knowledge to configure networks, manage users, set up firewalls, and implement security best practices.

As we progress, we will examine how Linux seamlessly integrates with cloud computing, empowering you to deploy applications and infrastructure on major cloud platforms. You will learn to navigate the world of open-source projects, contribute to their success, and gain insights from real-world case studies and interviews with experienced developers.

Throughout this book, our goal is to provide you with practical examples, clear explanations, and hands-on exercises that will solidify your understanding and enable you to apply your newfound knowledge effectively. By the end of this journey, you will be equipped with the skills and confidence to unlock the potential of Linux and open-source tools, unleashing your creativity and propelling your development endeavors to new heights.

So, whether you are a developer, system administrator, or tech enthusiast, let's embark on this Linux adventure together and unlock the limitless possibilities that open-source tools offer. Let's dive into "Linux for Developers: Unlocking the Potential of Open-Source Tools" and embark on a transformative journey into the world of Linux and its vast ecosystem.

Chapter 1: Introduction to Linux and Open Source

In this chapter, we lay the foundation for our exploration of Linux and open-source software. We delve into the evolution and history of Linux, understanding its significance in the technology landscape. We also uncover the philosophy behind open-source software and the benefits it offers to developers and users alike. By the end of this chapter, you will have a solid understanding of Linux, its key distributions, and the principles that drive the open-source movement. Get ready to unlock the potential of Linux and embrace the power of open-source tools.

1.1 Evolution and history of Linux

In this section, we delve into the evolution and history of Linux, tracing its origins and understanding how it has evolved into the powerful and widely-used operating system it is today.

The Origins of Unix:

We start by exploring the roots of Linux in the Unix operating system. Unix was developed in the late 1960s at Bell Labs and became widely used in academic and research institutions. It introduced concepts like multi-user access, file system organization, and a command-line interface, which laid the foundation for subsequent operating systems, including Linux.

The Birth of Linux:

We then dive into the story of Linux's birth. In 1991, a Finnish computer science student named Linus Torvalds started developing an operating system as a hobby project. He released the initial version, which consisted of a kernel, to the online community. This kernel formed the core of what would become Linux. Torvalds adopted the open-source philosophy, inviting others to contribute to the project and share their improvements.

Growth and Expansion:

We explore how Linux gained traction and grew in popularity throughout the 1990s. As more developers and enthusiasts contributed to the project, Linux evolved rapidly, benefiting from a collaborative and decentralized development model. Its versatility, stability, and ability to run on various hardware architectures attracted the attention of businesses and organizations.

The Rise of Distributions:

We discuss the concept of Linux distributions, which are complete operating system packages that include the Linux kernel along with additional software and utilities. We examine popular distributions such as Debian, Red Hat, Ubuntu, and SUSE. Each distribution tailors the Linux experience to meet specific needs, targeting different user groups ranging from beginners to advanced users and enterprise environments.

Linux in the Enterprise:

We highlight the growing adoption of Linux in the enterprise sector. Businesses recognized the advantages of Linux, including its reliability, security, and cost-effectiveness. Linux became the foundation for servers, powering a significant portion of internet infrastructure, cloud computing platforms, and supercomputers. Its open-source nature allowed businesses to customize and tailor Linux to their specific requirements.

Linux in Mobile and Embedded Systems:

We touch upon the expansion of Linux into the mobile and embedded systems markets. The development of Linux-based operating systems, such as Android, revolutionized the smartphone industry, making Linux a dominant player in the mobile ecosystem. Additionally, Linux's adaptability and efficiency made it ideal for powering embedded systems, such as routers, set-top boxes, and Internet of Things (IoT) devices.

By understanding the evolution and history of Linux, you gain insight into its origins, development model, and the philosophy that drives its success. Linux's journey from a student project to a globally adopted operating system showcases the power of open-source collaboration and the impact it can have on the software industry.

1.2 The philosophy behind open-source software

In this section, we explore the philosophy that underlies open-source software, including Linux, and how it has shaped the development and adoption of these projects.

The Concept of Open Source:

We start by introducing the concept of open-source software. Open-source refers to a type of software whose source code is freely available, allowing users to view, modify, and distribute it. Unlike proprietary software, which is controlled by a single entity, open-source software encourages collaboration and community involvement.

The Four Pillars of Open Source:

We delve into the four key pillars that define the open-source philosophy:

a. **Free Redistribution**: Open-source software permits the unrestricted distribution of the software, allowing users to share it with others without any limitations or fees.

b. **Source Code Access**: Open-source software provides access to its source code, allowing users to examine how the software works, make modifications, and contribute improvements.

c. **Derived Works**: Open-source licenses permit users to create and distribute modified versions of the software, promoting innovation and customization.

d. **Collaboration and Community**: Open-source projects thrive on collaboration and community involvement. Users are encouraged to contribute their knowledge, skills, and feedback to enhance the software and foster a supportive community.

Benefits of Open Source:

We discuss the numerous benefits of open-source software:

a.   **Transparency**:   Open-source   software's transparency allows users to verify its security, privacy, and functionality. Any vulnerabilities or bugs can be identified and resolved collaboratively.

b. **Flexibility and Customization**: Users have the freedom to modify the software to suit their specific needs, enabling customization and adaptability.

c. **Lower Costs**: Open-source software is often available at no cost, reducing licensing fees and promoting cost-effectiveness.

d.   **Rapid   Innovation   and   Improvement**:   The open-source   community   fosters   a   collaborative environment,   where   developers   from   diverse backgrounds contribute their expertise, resulting in rapid innovation and continuous improvement.

Open Source and the Developer Community:

We   highlight   the   significance   of   the   developer community   in   open-source   software.   Developers actively   engage   with   open-source   projects, contributing code, reporting bugs, and providing support to fellow users. This collective effort fuels the growth and success of open-source software.

By understanding the philosophy behind open-source software,   you   gain   insights   into   the   values   of collaboration,   transparency,   and   community-driven development. These principles have been instrumental in the success and widespread adoption of projects like Linux, empowering developers to leverage open-source tools and contribute to a vibrant ecosystem of innovation and collaboration.

1.3 Major Linux distributions and their characteristics

In this section, we explore some of the major Linux distributions and their unique characteristics. Linux distributions are complete operating system packages that include the Linux kernel, along with a selection of software, utilities, and package management systems.

Debian:

Debian is one of the oldest and most influential Linux distributions. It is known for its stability, reliability, and commitment to free and open-source software. Debian uses the Advanced Package Tool (APT) for package management, providing a vast repository of software packages. It offers different variants such as Debian GNU/Linux, Debian GNU/kFreeBSD, and Debian GNU/Hurd.

Ubuntu:

Ubuntu is a popular Linux distribution based on Debian. It focuses on usability, ease of installation, and a friendly user interface. Ubuntu has a large community and provides regular releases, including Long-Term Support (LTS) versions. It utilizes the APT package management system and features the Unity desktop environment (now transitioning to GNOME).

Fedora:

Fedora is a community-driven distribution sponsored by Red Hat. It emphasizes the use of cutting-edge technologies and serves as a testing ground for features that eventually make their way into Red Hat Enterprise Linux (RHEL). Fedora uses the DNF package manager and offers different desktop environments, including GNOME, KDE Plasma, Xfce, and more.

CentOS:

CentOS (Community Enterprise Operating System) is a distribution that aims to provide a free and open-source alternative to RHEL. It is known for its stability, long-term support, and compatibility with RHEL packages. CentOS follows the same package management system as RHEL, utilizing the YUM (Yellowdog Updater Modified) package manager.

Arch Linux:

Arch Linux is a lightweight and flexible distribution designed for users who prefer a do-it-yourself approach. It follows a rolling-release model, providing frequent updates and access to the latest software. Arch Linux uses the Pacman package manager and employs a simple, minimalistic philosophy, allowing users to build their system from the ground up.

openSUSE:

openSUSE is a community-driven distribution sponsored by SUSE. It offers a choice of stable and rolling-release editions, catering to different user preferences. openSUSE utilizes the Zypper package manager and supports multiple desktop environments, including GNOME, KDE Plasma, Xfce, and LXQt.

These are just a few examples of major Linux distributions, each with its own characteristics and target audience. Other notable distributions include Mint, Elementary OS, Gentoo, and Slackware. Exploring these distributions allows you to find the one that aligns with your needs and preferences, whether it be stability, ease of use, cutting-edge features, or customization options.

Chapter 2: Getting Started with Linux

In this chapter, we embark on our journey into the world of Linux. We guide you through the process of getting started with this powerful operating system, ensuring you have a solid foundation for your future endeavors. We explore different Linux distributions and help you choose the right one for your needs. From installation methods like dual-boot, virtual machines, or live USB, to mastering basic command-line operations, you will gain the essential skills required to navigate and work efficiently in a Linux environment. By the end of this chapter, you will be equipped with the necessary knowledge to confidently embark on your Linux journey and unlock its vast potential as a developer. Get ready to dive into the exciting world of Linux and unleash your creativity!

2.1 Choosing the right Linux distribution for your needs

In this section, we discuss important considerations to help you choose the right Linux distribution that aligns with your specific needs and requirements. With the wide variety of Linux distributions available, finding the one that suits you best can greatly enhance your overall Linux experience.

Purpose and Intended Use:

Consider the purpose for which you will be using Linux. Are you setting up a server, developing software, or using it as your primary desktop operating system? Different distributions excel in different areas, so identifying your primary use case will narrow down your options.

User Experience and Interface:

Evaluate the user experience and interface provided by various distributions. Some distributions, like Ubuntu and Linux Mint, prioritize a user-friendly experience with polished desktop environments, while others, like Arch Linux, offer a more minimalist and customizable approach. Consider your familiarity with Linux and your preferences regarding ease of use, aesthetics, and available software.

Hardware Compatibility:

Ensure that the distribution you choose is compatible with your hardware. Check for driver support and compatibility with your specific components, such as graphics cards, Wi-Fi adapters, and peripherals. Most major distributions provide hardware compatibility lists or forums where users can share their experiences.

Package Management:

Consider the package management system offered by each distribution. Package managers, such as APT, DNF, and Pacman, greatly impact how you install, update, and manage software. Evaluate the available software repositories, package availability, and ease of dependency resolution.

Community and Support:

Evaluate the size and activity of the distribution's community and support channels. A vibrant community can provide valuable resources, forums, and documentation to assist you in troubleshooting issues, learning new concepts, and finding answers to your questions.

Stability vs. Cutting-Edge:

Consider your preference for stability versus access to the latest software updates. Some distributions, like Debian and CentOS, prioritize stability and long-term support, making them suitable for production environments. On the other hand, distributions like Fedora and Arch Linux offer frequent updates and access to the latest software versions.

Customization and Flexibility:

Assess the level of customization and flexibility provided by each distribution. Some distributions, like Arch Linux and Gentoo, offer a more hands-on and do-it-yourself approach, allowing you to build a system tailored to your specific requirements. Others provide predefined desktop environments and configurations, suitable for users who prefer a more streamlined experience.

Remember that you can also experiment with different distributions by creating bootable USB drives or running them in virtual machines to get a feel for their features and usability before committing to an installation.

By considering these factors, you can choose a Linux distribution that aligns with your needs, preferences, and technical expertise. Remember that Linux offers a diverse ecosystem, ensuring that there's a distribution suitable for everyone, whether you're a beginner, power user, developer, or system administrator.

2.2 Installation methods: dual-boot, virtual machines, or live USB

In this section, we explore different installation methods for Linux, namely dual-booting, virtual machines, and using live USB drives. These methods allow you to run Linux alongside your existing operating system or in isolated environments without affecting your current setup.

Dual-Boot:

Dual-booting involves installing Linux alongside your existing operating system, allowing you to choose which one to boot into during system startup. Here's how it generally works:

a. **Prepare your system**: Create a separate partition on your hard drive to install Linux. Ensure you have enough free space and backup your important data.

b. **Download the Linux distribution**: Obtain the ISO file of the Linux distribution you wish to install. You can usually find it on the distribution's official website.

c. **Create a bootable USB or DVD**: Use a tool like Rufus or Etcher to create a bootable USB drive or burn the ISO file to a DVD.

d. **Install Linux**: Restart your computer and boot from the bootable USB or DVD. Follow the installation wizard to install Linux on the allocated partition. Choose the dual-boot option during installation.

e. **Choose the operating system**: After installation, each time you start your computer, you will be presented with a boot menu allowing you to select the operating system you want to use.

Dual-booting allows you to experience Linux directly on your hardware, providing full access to system resources and performance. However, it requires partitioning your hard drive and some technical know-how.

Virtual Machines:

Using virtual machines (VMs) allows you to run Linux within a virtualized environment on your existing operating system. This method offers flexibility and isolation. Here's a general outline of the process:

a. **Install a virtualization software**: Download and install a virtualization software like VirtualBox, VMware, or KVM.

b. **Create a virtual machine**: Create a new virtual machine within the virtualization software, specifying the desired hardware resources and allocating storage space.

c. **Install Linux on the virtual machine**: Use the downloaded Linux ISO file to install the Linux distribution on the virtual machine, following the installation wizard.

d. **Run Linux within the virtual machine**: Start the virtual machine, and it will boot into the Linux environment, running alongside your host operating system.

Running Linux in a virtual machine allows you to experiment with different distributions and configurations without affecting your main operating system. It provides an isolated environment, but keep in mind that performance may be slightly reduced compared to running Linux directly on your hardware.

Live USB:

A live USB allows you to run Linux directly from a USB drive without installing it on your computer. This method is handy for trying out Linux or troubleshooting issues. Here's a general process:

a. **Create a bootable USB**: Use a tool like Rufus or Etcher to create a bootable USB drive with the Linux distribution's ISO file.

b. **Boot from the USB**: Restart your computer and boot from the USB drive. Most computers have a boot menu accessible by pressing a specific key during startup (e.g., F12 or Esc).

c. **Run Linux from the USB**: The Linux distribution will load into a live environment, allowing you to explore the features and functionality without affecting your existing system.

Running Linux from a live USB provides a portable and temporary Linux environment. However, keep in mind that any changes or data created during the live session will not persist after rebooting.

These installation methods offer flexibility and options to explore Linux based on your needs and preferences. Dual-booting allows direct access to system resources, virtual machines provide isolation, and live USB drives offer portability. Choose the method that suits your requirements and enjoy the Linux experience!

2.3 Basic command-line operations: navigating, file and directory management

In this section, we dive into basic command-line operations, which are essential for navigating the Linux file system, managing files and directories, and performing common tasks efficiently.

Navigating the File System:

1. **pwd** : Print the current working directory.
2. **ls** : List files and directories in the current directory.
3. **cd** : Change directory. Use cd <directory> to move to a specific directory.

4. **cd ..** : Move up one level in the directory hierarchy.
5. **cd ~:** Move to the home directory.

File and Directory Management:

1. **mkdir**: Create a new directory. Use mkdir <directory> to create a directory with a specific name.
2. **touch**: Create an empty file. Use touch <filename> to create a file with a specific name.
3. **cp**: Copy files and directories. Use cp <source> <destination> to copy a file or directory.
4. **mv**: Move or rename files and directories. Use mv <source> <destination> to move a file or directory to a new location or rename it.
5. **rm**: Remove files and directories. Use rm <file> to delete a file, and rm -r <directory> to remove a directory and its contents recursively.
6. **ls -l**: List files and directories in a detailed format, showing permissions, ownership, size, and modification times.

Additional Command-Line Operations:

1. **cat**: Display the contents of a file.
2. **less**: Display the contents of a file, allowing scrolling and navigation.

3. **grep**: Search for a specific pattern or text within files.
4. **chmod**: Change the permissions of a file or directory.
5. **chown**: Change the ownership of a file or directory.
6. **man**: Access the manual pages for a command to get detailed information and usage instructions.

Remember to exercise caution when using command-line operations, especially when deleting files or directories, as these actions cannot be undone. It's always recommended to double-check your commands before executing them.

By mastering these basic command-line operations, you'll be able to navigate through the file system, create, copy, move, and delete files and directories efficiently, and perform various tasks from the command line, enhancing your productivity and control over your Linux system.

Chapter 3: Shell Scripting and Automation

In this chapter, we dive into the world of shell scripting and automation, empowering you to streamline your workflows and automate repetitive tasks. We begin by introducing you to different shells, such as Bash and Zsh, and help you understand their syntax and capabilities. You will learn how to work with variables, conditionals, and loops in shell scripts, allowing you to create powerful and flexible automation solutions. With practical examples and hands-on exercises, you will develop the skills to write scripts that save you time and effort.

Whether you want to automate file operations, perform system administration tasks, or build complex workflows, shell scripting will become an invaluable tool in your arsenal. By the end of this chapter, you will have a solid foundation in shell scripting and automation, unlocking new levels of efficiency and productivity in your development journey. Get ready to harness the power of scripting and take control of your Linux environment!

3.1 Introduction to different shells (Bash, Zsh, etc.)

In this section, we introduce different shells commonly used in Linux, such as Bash, Zsh, and others. The shell is a command-line interpreter that allows interaction with the operating system and execution of commands. Let's explore some popular shells:

Bash (Bourne Again Shell):

Bash is the default and most widely used shell in Linux distributions. It is highly compatible with the original Unix shell (sh) and provides numerous features for scripting and interactive use. Bash supports command history, tab completion, variables, control structures, functions, and more. Its scripting capabilities make it a powerful choice for automation and system administration tasks.

Zsh (Z Shell):

Zsh is an extended and highly customizable shell that offers additional features and improvements over Bash. It provides an interactive mode with enhanced command line editing, spelling correction, globbing, and powerful customization options. Zsh supports advanced plugins, themes, and configuration frameworks like Oh My Zsh, making it popular among power users and developers.

Fish (Friendly Interactive Shell):

Fish is a user-friendly shell with a focus on simplicity and discoverability. It offers a clean and intuitive interface with features like syntax highlighting, auto-suggestions, and a helpful web-based configuration tool. Fish aims to provide a more beginner-friendly and interactive experience while still supporting scripting capabilities.

Tcsh (TENEX C Shell):

Tcsh is an enhanced version of the C shell (csh) with additional features and improvements. It offers a C-like syntax, command-line editing, history substitutions, and job control. Tcsh is commonly used in the Unix world and provides a comfortable environment for interactive use.

Ksh (Korn Shell):

Ksh is a powerful shell that combines features from the Bourne shell (sh) and the C shell (csh). It offers advanced scripting capabilities, including arithmetic operations, advanced flow control, and built-in string manipulation. Ksh is known for its efficiency and compatibility with various Unix systems.

It's important to note that the choice of shell is largely a matter of personal preference and specific requirements. Bash is widely supported and recommended for beginners and general-purpose scripting, while Zsh, Fish, Tcsh, and Ksh cater to specific user preferences and use cases.

To switch between shells, you can use the chsh command (change shell) to modify your default shell. Each shell has its own configuration files, such as .bashrc for Bash and .zshrc for Zsh, where you can customize and set environment variables, aliases, and functions.

Exploring different shells and their features allows you to find the one that suits your needs, enhances your productivity, and provides a comfortable command-line experience in Linux.

3.2 Variables, conditionals, and loops in shell scripting

In this section, we delve into the fundamental concepts of variables, conditionals, and loops in shell scripting. These elements enable you to create powerful and dynamic scripts for automating tasks and executing complex operations.

Variables:

Variables in shell scripting are used to store and manipulate data. They are represented by names and can hold different types of values, such as numbers, strings, or arrays. Here are the basic operations related to variables:

- **Variable Assignment**: Assign a value to a variable using the = operator. For example: name="John"
- **Variable Access**: Retrieve the value of a variable by prefixing it with the $ sign. For example: echo $name
- **Variable Substitution**: Use the value of a variable within a string by enclosing it in double quotes. For example: echo "My name is $name"

Conditionals:

Conditionals allow you to make decisions and execute different actions based on certain conditions. The most commonly used conditional constructs in shell scripting are:

if statements: Execute a block of code if a certain condition is true. For example:

```
if [ condition ]; then
  # code to execute when the condition is true
fi
```

else statements: Execute a block of code if the preceding if condition is false. For example:

```
if [ condition ]; then
  # code to execute when the condition is true
else
  # code to execute when the condition is false
fi
```

elif statements: Check additional conditions if the preceding if or elif conditions are false. For example:

```
if [ condition1 ]; then
  # code to execute when condition1 is true
elif [ condition2 ]; then
  # code to execute when condition2 is true
else
  # code to execute when all conditions are false
fi
```

Loops:

Loops enable repetitive execution of code blocks. They help automate tasks that require iterating over a set of values or performing actions until a certain condition is met. Shell scripting provides different types of loops:

for loops: Iterate over a list of values or elements. For example:

```
for item in list; do
  # code to execute for each item in the list
done
```

while loops: Execute a block of code as long as a specified condition is true. For example:

```
while [ condition ]; do
  # code to execute while the condition is true
done
```

until loops: Execute a block of code until a specified condition becomes true. For example:

```
until [ condition ]; do
  # code to execute until the condition is true
done
```

These constructs provide the building blocks for creating dynamic and interactive shell scripts. By utilizing variables, conditionals, and loops, you can perform complex operations, make decisions based on specific conditions, and automate repetitive tasks in your scripts.

Note: Shell scripting syntax may vary slightly between different shells. Ensure to refer to the documentation specific to the shell you are using for accurate syntax and usage details.

3.3 Writing scripts for automating repetitive tasks

In this section, we explore the process of writing scripts to automate repetitive tasks using shell scripting. Automation allows you to save time and effort by creating scripts that execute a series of commands automatically. Here are the key steps to follow when writing scripts for automation:

Plan and Define the Task:

Identify the repetitive task you want to automate. Break it down into smaller steps and determine the inputs, outputs, and desired outcome. Consider the commands, conditionals, loops, and variables required to accomplish the task efficiently.

Create a New Shell Script:

Open a text editor and create a new file with a .sh extension. This file will contain your shell script. Begin the script with a shebang line, which specifies the shell interpreter to use. For example:

#!/bin/bash

Add Comments and Documentation:

Include comments at the beginning of the script to explain its purpose, usage, and any prerequisites. Comments help you and others understand the script's functionality and make future modifications easier.

Define Variables:

Declare variables that will store values used throughout the script. Assign appropriate values to the variables based on the task's requirements. For example:

```
# Variables
input_dir="/path/to/input"
output_dir="/path/to/output"
```

Write the Script Logic:

Utilize conditionals, loops, and commands to implement the desired functionality. Use variables to store and manipulate data as needed. Consider error handling and feedback to provide informative output during script execution.

Test and Debug:

Before deploying the script, test it thoroughly to ensure it performs as intended. Run the script with different inputs and scenarios, and verify that it produces the desired results. Debug any issues that arise by checking for syntax errors, incorrect commands, or unexpected behavior.

Make the Script Executable:

To run the script directly from the command line, make it executable using the chmod command. For example:

chmod +x script.sh

Execute the Script:

Execute the script by typing its name preceded by ./ in the terminal. For example:

./script.sh

Iterate and Improve:

Review the script's performance and seek opportunities for optimization. Refine the script by adding error handling, improving efficiency, or enhancing functionality based on feedback and evolving requirements.

By following these steps, you can create powerful shell scripts that automate repetitive tasks, saving time and effort. Shell scripting allows you to streamline your workflows, increase productivity, and focus on more complex or critical aspects of your work.

Chapter 4: Package Management

In this chapter, we explore the world of package management in Linux, a crucial aspect of software development and system administration. We delve into the different package management systems used in various Linux distributions, such as APT, YUM, and others, and help you understand their functionalities and workflows. You will learn how to manage software repositories, install, update, and remove packages, and handle dependencies effectively.

Mastering package management enables you to easily access and install a vast range of software libraries, frameworks, and applications, accelerating your development process. We provide practical examples and guide you through the common package management tasks you'll encounter in your Linux journey. By the end of this chapter, you will have the skills and knowledge to navigate package management systems confidently, ensuring a smooth and efficient development experience. Get ready to harness the power of package management and unlock a world of possibilities in your Linux environment!

4.1 Introduction to package managers: APT, YUM, and others

In this section, we introduce package managers, which are essential tools for managing software packages in Linux distributions. Package managers simplify the installation, updating, and removal of software, handling dependencies and ensuring system stability. Let's explore two popular package managers: APT (Advanced Package Tool) and YUM (Yellowdog Updater, Modified), along with others commonly used in different Linux distributions.

APT (Advanced Package Tool):

APT is the package manager used in Debian-based distributions, including Ubuntu and Linux Mint. It provides a powerful and user-friendly command-line interface for managing packages. APT uses a package repository system, where software packages are stored and can be easily accessed for installation or update. Key APT commands include:

- **apt-get**: Command-line tool for package management operations like installing, updating, and removing packages.
- **apt-cache**: Tool for querying information about packages available in the repositories.
- **apt-add-repository**: Command to add third-party repositories to the system.

YUM (Yellowdog Updater, Modified):

YUM is the default package manager for Red Hat-based distributions, including Fedora, CentOS, and RHEL (Red Hat Enterprise Linux). It simplifies the installation and management of software packages by automatically handling dependencies. YUM uses software repositories to store packages and resolve dependencies during installation. Key YUM commands include:

- **yum**: Command-line tool for package management, allowing operations like installation, updating, and removal.
- **yum search**: Command to search for packages by name or keywords.
- **yum update**: Command to update installed packages to their latest versions.

Other Package Managers:

While APT and YUM are widely used, other package managers are specific to certain Linux distributions:

- **Pacman**: The package manager used in Arch Linux and its derivatives, offering a straightforward command-line interface and a rolling-release model.
- **Zypper**: The package manager used in openSUSE and SUSE Linux Enterprise,

providing features like dependency resolution and system management capabilities.

- **DNF (Dandified YUM):** A next-generation package manager that replaces YUM in newer versions of Fedora and CentOS, offering improved performance and better dependency management.

It's important to note that different package managers have their own commands and package formats, but they serve the common purpose of simplifying software management. Understanding the package manager specific to your Linux distribution is crucial for efficient software installation, updates, and maintenance.

Package managers play a vital role in maintaining system integrity, managing software versions, and ensuring a stable and secure Linux environment. Mastering their usage empowers you to install and manage a wide range of software packages with ease.

4.2 Managing software repositories

In this section, we explore the management of software repositories, which are central to package management in Linux distributions. Software repositories contain collections of software packages that can be easily accessed and installed using a package manager. Here are the key aspects of managing software repositories:

Repository Types:

Linux distributions typically have different types of repositories:

Official Repositories: These repositories are maintained and supported by the distribution's developers. They contain a wide range of software packages that are thoroughly tested and verified for compatibility with the distribution.

Third-Party Repositories: These repositories are created and maintained by individuals or organizations outside the official distribution. They provide additional software packages that may not be available in the official repositories.

Repository Configuration Files:

Repository information is stored in configuration files on the Linux system. These files define the repository's location, URL, enabled status, and other relevant details. The configuration files can typically be found in the /etc/apt/sources.list directory for APT-based systems or /etc/yum.repos.d/ directory for YUM-based systems.

Adding Repositories:

To add a new repository, you need to modify the repository configuration file. You can manually edit the file using a text editor or use specific package manager commands to add repositories. For example:

- **APT**: Use the apt-add-repository command followed by the repository URL or PPA (Personal Package Archive) name.
- **YUM**: Create a new repository configuration file in the /etc/yum.repos.d/ directory, specifying the repository details.

Enabling and Disabling Repositories:

You can enable or disable repositories based on your requirements. Enabling a repository allows the package manager to access and install packages from that repository. Conversely, disabling a repository restricts the package manager from using it. Depending on the package manager, specific commands or configuration changes are used to enable or disable repositories.

Refreshing Repository Metadata:

After adding or modifying repositories, it is necessary to update the package manager's repository metadata. This metadata contains information about available packages, their versions, and dependencies. To refresh the repository metadata, use the appropriate command for your package manager:

APT: Use the apt-get update command.

YUM: Use the yum makecache or yum check-update command.

Managing Repository Priority:

In cases where multiple repositories provide the same package, you can set priority rules to determine which repository takes precedence. This ensures that the package manager installs the desired version from the preferred repository. The configuration for repository priority may vary depending on the package manager and distribution.

Removing Repositories:

To remove a repository, you need to modify the repository configuration file and delete the corresponding repository entry. Alternatively, package manager commands can be used to remove repositories.

Proper management of software repositories allows you to access a diverse range of software packages and keep your system up to date with the latest releases. It also enables you to leverage third-party repositories for additional software options. However, it's important to exercise caution when using third-party repositories and ensure they come from trusted sources to maintain system security and stability.

4.3 Installing, updating, and removing packages

In this section, we explore the essential operations of package management: installing, updating, and removing software packages using package managers in Linux distributions. These operations allow you to maintain your system's software in a well-managed and up-to-date state.

Installing Packages:

Package installation involves adding new software to your Linux system. To install a package, use the appropriate command for your package manager:

- **APT**: Use the apt-get install command followed by the package name. For example: apt-get install package-name
- **YUM**: Use the yum install command followed by the package name. For example: yum install package-name

Updating Packages:

Package updates ensure that you have the latest versions of installed software, which often include bug fixes, security patches, and new features. To update packages, use the respective command for your package manager:

APT: Use the apt-get update command to refresh the package repository metadata, followed by the apt-get upgrade command to perform the actual updates. For example:

apt-get update
apt-get upgrade

YUM: Use the yum update command to update installed packages to their latest versions. For example: yum update

Removing Packages:

Removing packages involves uninstalling software from your system. This can be done using the package manager's removal command:

- **APT**: Use the apt-get remove command followed by the package name. For example: apt-get remove package-name

- **YUM**: Use the yum remove command followed by the package name. For example: yum remove package-name

Dependency Handling:

Package managers automatically handle dependencies, which are additional software packages required by the package you are installing or updating. When you install or update a package, the package manager resolves dependencies and installs or updates them as necessary. This ensures that the software operates correctly and all its requirements are met.

Package Search:

Package managers provide search capabilities to help you find packages based on keywords or package names. This is useful when you want to discover new software or verify if a specific package is available. The search commands differ depending on the package manager:

- **APT**: Use the apt-cache search command followed by the keywords or package name. For example: apt-cache search keyword
- **YUM**: Use the yum search command followed by the keywords or package name. For example: yum search keyword

Package Information:

Package managers also offer commands to retrieve detailed information about installed or available packages. These commands provide details such as package version, description, dependencies, and more. The commands for retrieving package information vary between package managers:

- **APT**: Use the apt-cache show command followed by the package name. For example: apt-cache show package-name
- **YUM**: Use the yum info command followed by the package name. For example: yum info package-name

Properly managing package installation, updates, and removal ensures that your Linux system remains secure, stable, and up to date. Regularly updating packages and removing unnecessary ones can enhance system performance and security while providing access to the latest software releases and features.

Chapter 5: Version Control with Git

In this chapter, we delve into the world of version control with Git, an essential tool for modern software development. We begin by explaining the key concepts of distributed version control systems and how Git revolutionizes collaboration and code management. You will learn how to set up Git, configure it with your global settings, and create and manage repositories.

We guide you through fundamental Git operations, such as cloning repositories, committing changes, branching, and merging. You will gain an understanding of how branches and tags work, enabling you to organize and track different versions of your codebase effectively. Additionally, we explore remote repositories and collaboration workflows using platforms like GitHub or GitLab.

Through practical examples and hands-on exercises, you will develop the skills to leverage Git's power to track changes, collaborate with others, and effectively manage your codebase. By the end of this chapter, you will be equipped with the knowledge and confidence to make Git an integral part of your development workflow, unlocking new levels of productivity and efficiency in your projects. Get ready to master Git and take control of your code versioning like a pro!

5.1 Understanding Git's distributed version control system

In this section, we delve into the fundamental concepts of Git, a widely used distributed version control system. Git revolutionized the way developers collaborate on projects and track changes to their codebases. Understanding Git's distributed nature is essential for effectively utilizing its features. Let's explore the key aspects of Git's distributed version control system:

Centralized vs. Distributed Version Control:

Traditional version control systems, such as Subversion (SVN), follow a centralized model. They rely on a central server that stores the entire history of the codebase, and developers check out individual copies for making changes. In contrast, Git employs a distributed model where each user has a complete copy of the repository, including the entire history. This distributed approach offers several advantages, such as:

a. **Offline Work**: Developers can work on their local repositories, commit changes, and perform various operations without requiring a constant connection to a central server. This allows for seamless offline work and collaboration.

b. **Branching and Merging**: Git's distributed nature makes branching and merging fast and efficient. Developers can create multiple branches to work on different features or experiments independently, and later merge them back into the main codebase.

c. **Flexibility and Scalability**: Git's distributed system enables flexible workflows and decentralized collaboration. Developers can contribute to a project without being dependent on a single central authority, making it suitable for large-scale projects with distributed teams.

Local Repositories and Operations:

In Git, each user maintains a local repository that contains the entire history and metadata of the project. Users can perform various operations on their local repositories, such as creating commits, branching, merging, and exploring the project's history.

Remote Repositories:

Git also supports remote repositories hosted on servers or platforms like GitHub, GitLab, or Bitbucket. Remote repositories serve as a central point for sharing and collaborating on the codebase. Developers can push their local changes to a remote repository, fetch changes from the remote repository, and synchronize their work with others.

Cloning and Forking:

To start working with a Git project, developers can clone an existing repository. Cloning creates a local copy of the repository, allowing them to make changes and contribute to the project. Forking, specifically used in platforms like GitHub, creates a personal copy of a remote repository under a user's account, enabling them to work independently and propose changes through pull requests.

Collaboration and Pull Requests:

Git's distributed nature facilitates collaboration between developers. They can work on separate branches, make changes, and later merge their branches together. Pull requests are commonly used to propose changes to a project hosted on a remote repository. They provide a mechanism for code review, discussion, and integration of contributions.

Understanding Git's distributed version control system empowers developers to work efficiently, collaborate seamlessly, and maintain a complete history of their codebase. Whether working individually or as part of a team, Git's distributed model provides flexibility, scalability, and robust version control capabilities.

5.2 Setting up Git: configuration and global settings

In this section, we cover the initial setup of Git, including configuring Git and managing global settings. Proper configuration ensures that Git works seamlessly and aligns with your preferred workflow. Let's explore the essential steps for setting up Git:

Installing Git:

Before configuring Git, you need to install it on your system. Git is available for various operating systems, including Windows, macOS, and Linux. Visit the official Git website (https://git-scm.com) to download and install the appropriate version for your platform.

Configuring User Information:

Once Git is installed, the first configuration step is to set your user information, which includes your name and email address. Git uses this information to associate your commits with your identity. Use the following commands to configure your user information:

```
git config --global user.name "Your Name"
git       config       --global       user.email
"your-email@example.com"
```

Replace "Your Name" with your actual name and "your-email@example.com" with your email address.

Configuring Text Editors:

By default, Git uses the system's default text editor for commit messages and other Git operations. However, you can configure Git to use a different text editor of your choice. For example, if you prefer using Visual Studio Code as your text editor, you can set it as the default editor for Git with the following command:

```
git config --global core.editor "code --wait"
```

Replace "code" with the command that launches your preferred text editor.

Setting Up Global Settings:

Git provides a range of global settings that affect its behavior. Some commonly used global settings include:

Setting the default branch name (e.g., from "master" to "main"):

```
git config --global init.defaultBranch main
```

Enabling colored output for Git commands:

git config --global color.ui true

Configuring line ending conversions to handle platform-specific line endings:

git config --global core.autocrlf true # for Windows
git config --global core.autocrlf input # for macOS/Linux

These are just a few examples of global settings. You can explore additional settings in the Git documentation or by running git config --help.

By properly configuring Git and managing global settings, you ensure that Git operates according to your preferences and aligns with your workflow. These initial setup steps provide a solid foundation for using Git effectively in version control and collaboration workflows.

5.3 Basic Git operations: cloning, committing, branching, merging

In this section, we explore the fundamental Git operations that form the backbone of version control and collaboration workflows. These operations include cloning repositories, creating commits, branching, and merging changes. Let's dive into the basic Git operations:

Cloning a Repository:

To start working with a Git project, you can clone an existing repository. Cloning creates a local copy of the repository on your machine, allowing you to make changes and contribute to the project. Use the following command to clone a repository:

git clone <repository URL>

Replace <repository URL> with the URL of the remote repository. Once cloned, you will have a complete local copy, including the entire history of the project.

Committing Changes:

Commits are at the heart of Git. A commit represents a snapshot of your codebase at a particular point in time. To commit changes, follow these steps:

a. **Stage Changes**: Use the git add command to stage files for the commit. For example:

git add file1.txt file2.txt

b. **Create a Commit**: Use the git commit command to create a commit with a meaningful message describing the changes. For example:

git commit -m "Add new feature"

Committing your changes records them in the repository's history, making them part of the project's timeline.

Branching:

Branching allows you to work on different features or experiments independently, keeping your changes separate from the main codebase until you are ready to merge them. To create a new branch, use the git branch command followed by the branch name. For example:

git branch new-feature

To switch to the newly created branch, use the git checkout command:

git checkout new-feature

Now you can make changes on the new branch without affecting the main branch.

Merging Changes:

Once you have made changes on a separate branch and tested them, you can merge those changes back into the main branch. The most common merge operation is the "fast-forward" merge, which occurs when the branch being merged has a linear history and is ahead of the main branch. Use the following commands to merge changes:

a. Switch to the main branch:

git checkout main

b. Merge the changes from the other branch:

git merge new-feature

Git will automatically merge the changes and create a new commit that incorporates both branches' histories.

These basic Git operations provide the foundation for version control and collaboration workflows. By cloning repositories, committing changes, creating branches, and merging them, you can effectively track and manage the evolution of your codebase while collaborating with others.

Chapter 6: Developing with Linux Tools

In this chapter, we explore the rich ecosystem of development tools available in the Linux environment. We dive into the world of integrated development environments (IDEs), command-line text editors, and debugging tools, empowering you to enhance your productivity and streamline your coding process.

We provide an overview of popular IDEs, such as Eclipse, Visual Studio Code, and others, highlighting their features and capabilities. You will learn how to set up and customize your IDE to suit your development needs and efficiently manage your projects.

Additionally, we delve into command-line text editors like Vim, Emacs, and Nano, which offer lightweight and powerful editing capabilities. We guide you through their usage, configuration, and essential productivity features, enabling you to navigate and edit code efficiently from the command line.

Debugging is a crucial aspect of software development, and we introduce you to essential debugging tools like GDB, Valgrind, and strace. You will learn how to utilize these tools to analyze and troubleshoot your code, allowing you to identify and fix bugs effectively.

Through practical examples and hands-on exercises, you will gain the skills to leverage these Linux development tools and take your coding abilities to new heights. By the end of this chapter, you will be equipped with the knowledge to choose and utilize the most suitable tools for your development workflow, unlocking your potential as a Linux developer. Get ready to embrace the power of Linux tools and elevate your coding experience!

6.1 Overview of popular IDEs: Eclipse, Visual Studio Code, etc.

In this section, we provide an overview of popular Integrated Development Environments (IDEs) that are widely used by developers working with Linux. IDEs are powerful tools that enhance productivity by providing a comprehensive development environment with features like code editing, debugging, version control integration, and more. Let's explore some of the popular IDEs used in Linux development:

Eclipse:

Eclipse is a versatile and extensible IDE that supports various programming languages, including Java, C/C++, Python, and more. It offers a rich set of features such as code auto-completion, refactoring tools, debugging capabilities, and integration with build systems. Eclipse also supports plugins that can be used to extend its functionality for specific development needs.

Visual Studio Code:

Visual Studio Code (VS Code) has gained immense popularity due to its lightweight yet powerful nature. It provides a modern and customizable user interface along with support for a wide range of programming languages. VS Code offers features like intelligent code completion, debugging, built-in Git integration, and an extensive marketplace for extensions. It is highly extensible and can be customized to suit individual preferences and development workflows.

IntelliJ IDEA:

IntelliJ IDEA is a feature-rich IDE primarily focused on Java development. It offers advanced coding assistance, code analysis, and refactoring capabilities. IntelliJ IDEA also supports other languages such as Kotlin, JavaScript, Python, and more. It provides integration with popular build tools and version control systems, making it a popular choice for Java developers.

Atom:

Atom is an open-source text editor developed by GitHub. Although Atom is not a full-fledged IDE, it can be customized and extended using packages to provide IDE-like features. It offers a clean and intuitive interface, supports multiple programming languages, and provides features like code highlighting, Git integration, and a built-in package manager.

Sublime Text:

Sublime Text is a lightweight and fast text editor with a minimalistic design. It supports various programming languages and offers a wide range of features like multiple cursors, split editing, powerful search and replace, and customizable key bindings. Sublime Text has a large and active user community that creates plugins and extensions to enhance its functionality.

NetBeans:

NetBeans is an open-source IDE primarily focused on Java development but also supports other languages such as PHP, HTML, and more. It provides a comprehensive set of features for Java development, including code generation, debugging, refactoring tools, and integration with popular application servers. NetBeans has a user-friendly interface and supports plugin development.

These are just a few examples of popular IDEs used in Linux development. Each IDE has its strengths and unique features, catering to different programming languages and development requirements. It's essential to explore and try out different IDEs to find the one that best suits your needs and enhances your productivity as a Linux developer.

6.2 Command-line text editors: Vim, Emacs, Nano

In addition to IDEs, command-line text editors are powerful tools commonly used by Linux developers. These editors provide a lightweight and efficient way to edit code and text files directly from the terminal. Let's explore three popular command-line text editors used in Linux: Vim, Emacs, and Nano.

Vim:

Vim (Vi IMproved) is a highly configurable and feature-rich text editor that evolved from the classic Vi editor. It offers a modal editing interface with different modes for editing, navigation, and command execution. Vim is known for its extensive set of commands, customizable keybindings, and powerful editing capabilities. It supports syntax highlighting, code folding, split windows, macros, and plugins, making it a preferred choice for many experienced users.

Emacs:

Emacs is a versatile and extensible text editor that provides a wide range of features and functions beyond simple text editing. It offers a powerful Lisp-based scripting language that allows users to customize and extend its functionality. Emacs supports various programming languages, syntax highlighting, auto-completion, and integrated debugging. It also includes a range of additional features such as an integrated email client, web browser, and file manager.

Nano:

Nano is a user-friendly and straightforward command-line text editor designed for ease of use. It aims to provide a simple and accessible editing experience for both beginners and experienced users. Nano offers basic text editing features, including syntax highlighting, search and replace, line numbering, and multiple buffers. It presents a user-friendly interface with on-screen menus that display available commands and key combinations.

Each of these command-line text editors has its own strengths and learning curves. Vim and Emacs are highly customizable and offer extensive functionality once mastered, but they may have a steeper learning curve for beginners. On the other hand, Nano provides a more straightforward and beginner-friendly editing experience out of the box.

Choosing the right command-line text editor depends on personal preference, workflow, and familiarity with the editor's commands and capabilities. It's worth exploring and trying out different editors to find the one that best suits your needs and enhances your productivity in the Linux command-line environment.

6.3 Debugging tools: GDB, Valgrind, strace

Debugging is an essential part of the development process, allowing developers to identify and resolve issues in their code. Linux provides several powerful debugging tools that aid in the troubleshooting and analysis of programs. Let's explore three popular debugging tools used in Linux: GDB, Valgrind, and strace.

GDB (GNU Debugger):

GDB is a powerful command-line debugger that helps developers analyze and debug programs written in various programming languages, including C, C++, and Assembly. It allows you to set breakpoints, inspect variables, step through code, and track the flow of program execution. GDB provides a rich set of commands and features for debugging and is widely used in both command-line and IDE-based development workflows.

Valgrind:

Valgrind is a dynamic analysis tool that helps detect memory leaks, memory errors, and other runtime issues in programs. It operates as a virtual machine for your application, providing instrumentation and analysis of memory usage. Valgrind can identify problems such as invalid memory accesses, uninitialized variables, and memory leaks. It is particularly useful for identifying subtle memory-related bugs that may be challenging to detect through manual debugging.

Strace:

strace is a command-line tool that traces system calls and signals of a running program. It allows you to monitor and analyze the interactions between a program and the underlying operating system. strace can help you understand how your program is interacting with system resources, identify performance bottlenecks, and diagnose issues related to file I/O, network communication, and process management. It provides detailed information about system calls, signal handling, and resource usage.

Each of these debugging tools serves a specific purpose and can be valuable in different scenarios. GDB is ideal for interactive debugging and stepping through code, Valgrind helps identify memory-related issues, and strace is useful for monitoring system interactions. Depending on your specific debugging needs, you can choose the appropriate tool or combine them to gain deeper insights into your program's behavior.

Becoming familiar with these debugging tools and incorporating them into your development workflow can significantly enhance your ability to troubleshoot and resolve issues effectively, leading to more robust and reliable software.

Chapter 7: Web Development with Linux

In this chapter, we delve into the exciting world of web development with Linux as our platform of choice. We guide you through the process of setting up web servers, working with databases, and exploring various programming languages and frameworks.

We begin by discussing different web server options available on Linux, such as Apache, Nginx, and Lighttpd. You will learn how to install, configure, and secure these servers to host your web applications.

Next, we explore the fundamentals of databases and their integration with web development. We cover popular database systems like MySQL, PostgreSQL, and MongoDB, and guide you through the process of installing, configuring, and interacting with these databases using Linux tools.

To develop dynamic web applications, we explore various programming languages and frameworks, including PHP, Python with Django, and JavaScript with Node.js. You will learn how to set up development environments, work with frameworks, and build powerful web applications using these technologies.

Throughout this chapter, we provide practical examples and hands-on exercises to reinforce your understanding and enable you to apply your knowledge effectively. By the end of this chapter, you will have a solid foundation in web development with Linux, empowering you to create and deploy robust and dynamic web applications. Get ready to unleash your creativity and embark on an exciting web development journey with Linux!

7.1 Installing and configuring Apache or Nginx web servers

When it comes to web development on Linux, having a reliable web server is crucial. Two popular choices for web servers are Apache and Nginx. In this section, we'll explore how to install and configure these web servers on Linux.

Installing Apache:

- a. **Update Package Repositories**: Before installing Apache, it's recommended to update your package repositories to ensure you have the latest software available.
- b. **Install Apache**: Use your Linux distribution's package manager to install Apache. For example, on Ubuntu, you can run the command: sudo apt-get install apache2.

- c. **Start and Enable Apache**: Once installed, start the Apache service and enable it to start automatically on system boot. On Ubuntu, use the commands: sudo systemctl start apache2 and sudo systemctl enable apache2.
- d. **Test Apache**: Open a web browser and enter http://localhost or http://your_server_ip to verify that Apache is running correctly. You should see the default Apache welcome page.

Configuring Apache:

- a. **Configuration Files:** Apache's main configuration file is typically located at /etc/apache2/apache2.conf or a similar path depending on your distribution. Edit this file to make configuration changes.
- b. **Virtual Hosts**: Apache supports virtual hosts, allowing you to host multiple websites on the same server. Configure virtual hosts by creating separate configuration files for each site in the /etc/apache2/sites-available/ directory and enabling them with the a2ensite command.
- c. **Restart Apache**: After making changes to the Apache configuration, restart the service for the changes to take effect. Use the command: sudo systemctl restart apache2.

Installing Nginx:

- a. **Update Package Repositories**: Similar to Apache, update your package repositories before installing Nginx.
- b. **Install Nginx**: Use your package manager to install Nginx. For example, on Ubuntu, run: sudo apt-get install nginx.
- c. **Start and Enable Nginx**: Start the Nginx service and enable it to start automatically on system boot. On Ubuntu, use the commands: sudo systemctl start nginx and sudo systemctl enable nginx.
- d. **Test Nginx**: Similar to Apache, open a web browser and enter http://localhost or http://your_server_ip to verify that Nginx is running. You should see the default Nginx welcome page.

Configuring Nginx:

- a. **Configuration Files**: Nginx's main configuration file is usually located at /etc/nginx/nginx.conf. Edit this file to make configuration changes.
- b. **Server Blocks**: Nginx uses server blocks to define separate virtual hosts. Configure server blocks by creating separate configuration files in the /etc/nginx/sites-available/ directory and enabling them with symbolic links in the /etc/nginx/sites-enabled/ directory.
- c. **Restart Nginx**: After modifying the Nginx configuration, restart the service for the

changes to take effect. Use the command: sudo systemctl restart nginx.

By following these steps, you can successfully install and configure Apache or Nginx as your web server on Linux. Remember to consult the official documentation for your specific distribution if you encounter any issues or need more detailed instructions.

7.2 Database management with MySQL/MariaDB and PostgreSQL

Databases are integral to web development, providing a structured way to store and retrieve data for web applications. Two popular database management systems used in Linux are MySQL/MariaDB and PostgreSQL. In this section, we'll explore how to manage these databases on Linux.

Installing and Setting Up MySQL/MariaDB:

- a. **Update Package Repositories**: Before installing MySQL/MariaDB, update your package repositories to ensure you have the latest software available.
- b. **Install MySQL/MariaDB**: Use your distribution's package manager to install the MySQL/MariaDB server. For example, on

Ubuntu, you can run the command: sudo apt-get install mysql-server.

- c. **Secure the Installation**: After installation, run the security script provided by MySQL/MariaDB to secure your database installation. This script sets a root password, removes anonymous users, and disables remote root login.
- d. **Start and Enable the Service**: Start the MySQL/MariaDB service and enable it to start automatically on system boot. On Ubuntu, use the commands: sudo systemctl start mysql and sudo systemctl enable mysql.

Configuring MySQL/MariaDB:

- a. **Accessing MySQL/MariaDB**: To interact with MySQL/MariaDB, use the command-line client by running mysql -u root -p and entering the root password you set during installation. This gives you access to the MySQL/MariaDB prompt where you can execute SQL commands.
- b. **Creating Databases and Users**: Use SQL commands to create databases and users, grant privileges, and manage access to the databases. For example, to create a new database, use the command: CREATE DATABASE dbname;, and to create a new user and grant privileges, use: CREATE USER 'username'@'localhost' IDENTIFIED BY

'password'; GRANT ALL PRIVILEGES ON dbname.* TO 'username'@'localhost';.

- c. **Configuring Database Options**: MySQL/MariaDB provides a configuration file where you can fine-tune database settings. The location of the configuration file may vary depending on your distribution. Common locations include /etc/my.cnf or /etc/mysql/my.cnf. Edit this file to make configuration changes.

Installing and Setting Up PostgreSQL:

- a. **Update Package Repositories**: Before installing PostgreSQL, update your package repositories to ensure you have the latest software available.
- b. **Install PostgreSQL**: Use your distribution's package manager to install PostgreSQL. For example, on Ubuntu, run: sudo apt-get install postgresql.
- c. **Accessing PostgreSQL**: PostgreSQL creates a default user named "postgres" during installation. To access the PostgreSQL prompt, run: sudo -u postgres psql.
- d. **Create Databases and Users**: Use SQL commands within the PostgreSQL prompt to create databases and users. For example, to create a database, use the command: CREATE DATABASE dbname;, and to create a user with privileges, use: CREATE USER

username WITH ENCRYPTED PASSWORD 'password'; GRANT ALL PRIVILEGES ON DATABASE dbname TO username;.

Configuring PostgreSQL:

- a. **Configuration Files**: PostgreSQL's main configuration file is usually located at /etc/postgresql/<version>/main/postgresql.conf. Edit this file to make configuration changes.
- b. **Managing Connections**: PostgreSQL provides settings to control the number of simultaneous connections, memory usage, and other parameters. Adjust these settings according to your application's needs.
- c. **Restart PostgreSQL**: After making configuration changes, restart the PostgreSQL service for the changes to take effect. Use the command: sudo systemctl restart postgresql.

By following these steps, you can successfully install, configure, and manage MySQL/MariaDB and PostgreSQL databases on Linux. Each database management system offers its unique features, so consult their respective documentation for more detailed instructions and advanced usage.

7.3 PHP, Python, or Node.js development environments

To develop dynamic web applications, you'll need a programming language and a development environment that supports it. Three popular choices for web development on Linux are PHP, Python, and Node.js. In this section, we'll explore setting up development environments for each of these languages.

PHP Development Environment:

- a. **Install PHP**: Use your distribution's package manager to install PHP. For example, on Ubuntu, run: sudo apt-get install php.
- b. **Install a Web Server**: PHP requires a web server to run. As discussed earlier, you can install Apache or Nginx as your web server. Follow the instructions from Section 7.1 to install and configure the web server of your choice.
- c. **Install PHP Extensions**: Depending on your application's requirements, you may need to install additional PHP extensions. Use the package manager or PHP's package manager, such as pecl or composer, to install the necessary extensions.
- d. **Configure PHP**: PHP's configuration file is usually located at /etc/php/php.ini. Edit this file

to modify PHP settings such as error reporting, file upload limits, and more.

- e. **Test PHP**: Create a test PHP file, such as test.php, with some basic PHP code, like <?php phpinfo(); ?>. Place the file in your web server's document root directory and access it in a web browser (http://localhost/test.php) to verify that PHP is working correctly.

Python Development Environment:

- a. **Install Python**: Linux distributions typically come with Python pre-installed. However, you may need to install additional Python packages depending on your development needs. Use your package manager to install Python and related packages.
- b. **Choose a Python IDE or Text Editor**: There are several options for Python development environments, including IDEs like PyCharm, Visual Studio Code with Python extensions, or text editors like Sublime Text or Vim. Install your preferred development environment.
- c. **Virtual Environments**: It's recommended to use virtual environments to isolate Python project dependencies. Install virtualenv or venv and create a virtual environment for your project.
- d. **Install Python Packages**: Use pip, the Python package manager, to install required

packages for your project. Activate your virtual environment and run pip install package-name to install packages.

- e. **Test Python**: Create a Python script, such as test.py, with some sample code, and run it using the Python interpreter (python test.py) to ensure Python is working correctly.

Node.js Development Environment:

- a. **Install Node.js**: Node.js is typically installed through a package manager or by downloading the Node.js binary from the official website. Follow the installation instructions provided by the Node.js documentation for your Linux distribution.
- b. **Choose a Text Editor**: Node.js development can be done using any text editor. Popular choices include Visual Studio Code, Sublime Text, Atom, or Vim. Install your preferred text editor.
- c. **Package.json and npm**: Initialize a new Node.js project by creating a package.json file. Run npm init in your project directory and follow the prompts. This file will track your project's dependencies and other metadata.
- d. **Install Node.js Modules**: Use npm, the Node.js package manager, to install required modules for your project. Run npm install module-name to install modules specified in your package.json file.

- e. **Test Node.js:** Create a Node.js script, such as test.js, with some sample code, and run it using the Node.js interpreter (node test.js) to ensure Node.js is working correctly.

By following these steps, you can set up a development environment for PHP, Python, or Node.js on Linux. Choose the language that best fits your project's requirements and leverage the rich ecosystem of libraries, frameworks, and tools available for web development in each language.

Chapter 8: Containerization with Docker

In this chapter, we dive into the world of containerization with Docker, a revolutionary technology that has transformed software development and deployment. We guide you through the process of understanding and leveraging Docker to encapsulate your applications and streamline their deployment across environments.

We start by introducing the core concepts of containerization and the advantages it offers. You will learn how Docker simplifies the packaging, distribution, and deployment of applications by encapsulating them into lightweight and portable containers.

We guide you through the installation and configuration of Docker on your Linux system, ensuring you have the necessary tools to work with containers effectively. You will learn how to create and manage containers using Docker's command-line interface and explore the Dockerfile syntax to build custom container images.

We delve into container networking, data management, and orchestration using tools like Docker Compose and Docker Swarm. You will gain the skills to define multi-container applications, manage container interconnectivity, and scale your application across a cluster of machines.

Through practical examples and hands-on exercises, you will develop the expertise to leverage Docker to streamline your development workflow, enable reproducibility, and simplify deployment. By the end of this chapter, you will be equipped with the knowledge and confidence to harness the power of containerization with Docker, empowering you to build and deploy applications with ease. Get ready to embrace the future of software development and unlock new levels of efficiency with Docker!

8.1 Introduction to containers and containerization

Containerization is a popular approach in modern software development and deployment that allows applications to run reliably and consistently across different environments. Containers provide a lightweight and isolated runtime environment for applications, encapsulating all the dependencies and configurations needed to run the application smoothly. In this section, we'll explore the concept of containers and the benefits they offer.

What are Containers?

Containers are self-contained, portable units that package an application and its dependencies, including libraries, frameworks, and runtime environments. They provide an isolated and consistent environment for the application to run, regardless of the underlying host system. Containers utilize operating system-level virtualization to separate the application and its dependencies from the host system, ensuring that the application runs consistently across different environments.

Benefits of Containerization:

a. **Portability**: Containers are highly portable, allowing applications to run consistently across different environments, such as development machines, testing servers, and production systems. Containers eliminate the "works on my machine" problem by ensuring that the application behaves the same way across all environments.

b. **Isolation**: Containers provide isolation between applications and the host system. Each container operates independently, with its own file system, network stack, and process space. This isolation prevents conflicts between applications and improves security by limiting the impact of potential vulnerabilities.

c. **Resource Efficiency**: Containers are lightweight compared to traditional virtual machines since they share the host system's operating system kernel. This results in faster startup times and reduced resource consumption. Multiple containers can run on the same host without significant performance degradation.

d. **Scalability**: Containerization simplifies application scaling. Containers can be easily replicated and distributed across multiple hosts, enabling efficient horizontal scaling to handle increased workloads. Container orchestration tools like Kubernetes further simplify the management and scaling of containerized applications.

e. **DevOps Enablement**: Containerization aligns well with DevOps practices, enabling faster and more efficient software development, deployment, and continuous integration/continuous deployment (CI/CD) pipelines. Containers facilitate the creation of reproducible development environments, seamless deployment of applications, and easy rollbacks.

Container Runtimes:

Container runtimes are responsible for managing and executing containers. Docker is one of the most widely used container runtimes, providing a user-friendly interface and a rich ecosystem of tools and services. Other container runtimes include containerd, rkt, and Podman, each with its own set of features and capabilities.

Container Images:

Containers are created from container images, which are read-only snapshots of an application and its dependencies. Container images are built using Dockerfiles or other container image specifications and can be easily shared and distributed. Container registries, such as Docker Hub or private registries, serve as repositories for storing and retrieving container images.

In conclusion, containerization revolutionizes software development and deployment by providing a lightweight, portable, and isolated runtime environment for applications. Containers offer numerous benefits, including portability, isolation, resource efficiency, scalability, and DevOps enablement. By leveraging container runtimes and container images, developers can build and deploy applications that run consistently across different environments.

8.2 Installing Docker and managing Docker images

To start containerizing your applications with Docker, you'll need to install Docker on your Linux system and familiarize yourself with managing Docker images. In this section, we'll cover the installation process and basic operations for managing Docker images.

Installing Docker:

- a. **Check System Requirements**: Ensure that your Linux system meets the minimum requirements for running Docker. Visit the official Docker documentation for specific details on system requirements.
- b. **Installation Method**: Docker provides various installation methods for different Linux distributions. You can choose to install Docker using the official repositories, package managers, or by downloading the Docker binary from the official website. Follow the installation instructions provided by Docker for your specific Linux distribution.

Docker Daemon:

Once Docker is installed, the Docker daemon, a background service, will start running on your system. The Docker daemon is responsible for managing Docker containers and images. You can interact with Docker through the command-line interface (CLI) or use graphical user interfaces (GUI) tools.

Docker Images:

Docker images serve as the building blocks for containers. They are read-only snapshots that include the application, its dependencies, and the instructions to run it. To manage Docker images, you'll perform the following operations:

a. **Searching for Images**: Use the docker search command to search the Docker Hub registry for available images. For example, docker search nginx will search for NGINX-related images.

b. **Pulling Images**: Use the docker pull command to download Docker images from a registry. For example, docker pull nginx will download the latest NGINX image.

c. **Listing Images**: Use the docker images command to list the Docker images available on your system.

d. **Tagging Images**: Use the docker tag command to assign tags or labels to images, making them easier to identify and reference. For example, docker tag nginx myrepo/nginx will tag the NGINX image as myrepo/nginx.

e. **Pushing Images**: Use the docker push command to upload your tagged images to a registry. For example, docker push myrepo/nginx will push the tagged NGINX image to the myrepo repository.

f. **Removing Images**: Use the docker rmi command to remove unwanted or unused images from your local system. For example, docker rmi nginx will remove the NGINX image from your system.

Docker Registry:

Docker Hub is the default public registry for Docker images, but you can also use private registries for storing and sharing images. Docker Hub allows you to create your own repositories or use existing repositories to host and distribute Docker images. Private registries provide additional control and security for your images.

By installing Docker and mastering the basics of managing Docker images, you'll be ready to create, deploy, and distribute containerized applications with ease. Docker's extensive ecosystem and vast collection of images make it a powerful tool for containerization and software development.

8.3 Creating, running, and deploying containers with Docker

Once you have Docker installed and Docker images available, you can start creating, running, and deploying containers. In this section, we'll explore the basic operations for working with Docker containers.

Creating Containers:

- a. **Creating Containers from Images**: Use the docker create command to create a container from a Docker image. For example, docker create --name mycontainer nginx will create a container named "mycontainer" from the NGINX image.
- b. **Configuring Containers**: Containers can be configured with various options, such as specifying environment variables, exposing ports, mounting volumes, and linking containers together. Use the appropriate flags with the docker create command to customize the container's behavior.

Running Containers:

a. **Starting Containers**: Use the docker start command to start a stopped container. For example, docker start mycontainer will start the "mycontainer" container.

b. Stopping Containers: Use the docker stop command to stop a running container. For example, docker stop mycontainer will stop the "mycontainer" container gracefully.

c. **Restarting Containers**: Use the docker restart command to restart a stopped container. For example, docker restart mycontainer will restart the "mycontainer" container.

d. **Listing Containers**: Use the docker ps command to list the running containers on your system. Adding the -a flag (docker ps -a) will list all containers, including the stopped ones.

e. **Removing Containers**: Use the docker rm command to remove a stopped container. For example, docker rm mycontainer will remove the "mycontainer" container.

Deploying Containers:

- a. **Container Networking**: Docker provides networking capabilities to enable communication between containers and the host system or other containers. You can configure container networking using options like port mapping, linking, and creating user-defined networks.

- b. **Container Orchestration**: For larger-scale deployments, container orchestration tools like Kubernetes, Docker Swarm, or Apache Mesos can be used to manage and scale containerized applications across multiple hosts. These tools automate the deployment, scaling, and management of containers, providing advanced features like load balancing, service discovery, and high availability.

- c. **Docker Compose**: Docker Compose is a tool that allows you to define and manage multi-container applications using a YAML file. It simplifies the deployment of interconnected containers and provides a declarative way to specify container configurations, volumes, and networking.

Monitoring and Troubleshooting:

Docker provides various commands and tools to monitor and troubleshoot containers. The docker logs command displays the logs of a running container, helping you troubleshoot any issues. Additionally, you can use tools like docker stats to monitor resource usage of running containers, docker exec to execute commands inside a running container, and docker inspect to get detailed information about a container.

By mastering the creation, running, and deployment of containers with Docker, you can harness the power of containerization to build scalable and portable applications. Docker's flexibility, portability, and robust ecosystem make it a popular choice for containerization in both development and production environments.

Chapter 9: Linux Networking

In this chapter, we explore the essential aspects of networking in a Linux environment. Networking forms a crucial foundation for various applications and services, and understanding its principles and configurations is essential for developers.

We start by covering the basics of network architecture, protocols, and addressing schemes. You will gain a solid understanding of IP addressing, subnetting, and routing, enabling you to configure and troubleshoot network connectivity effectively.

We delve into configuring network interfaces, both physical and virtual, and explore tools and commands to manage network settings. You will learn how to set up IP addresses, configure DNS, handle network services, and troubleshoot common network issues.

We also dive into firewall management and security, exploring the Linux netfilter framework and tools like iptables and firewalld. You will learn how to define and implement firewall rules to control network traffic and protect your systems.

Additionally, we cover network troubleshooting techniques, examining tools like ping, traceroute, and tcpdump. You will learn how to use these tools to diagnose and resolve network connectivity issues effectively.

Throughout this chapter, we provide practical examples and hands-on exercises to reinforce your understanding and help you apply your networking knowledge in real-world scenarios. By the end of this chapter, you will have a solid foundation in Linux networking, empowering you to configure, troubleshoot, and secure network connections in your applications and systems. Get ready to master Linux networking and optimize your network infrastructure!

9.1 Networking fundamentals: IP addresses, DNS, and routing

In this section, we'll explore the fundamentals of networking in Linux, including IP addresses, DNS (Domain Name System), and routing. Understanding these concepts is crucial for effectively configuring and managing network connections on your Linux system.

IP Addresses:

- a. **IPv4 and IPv6**: IP (Internet Protocol) addresses are unique identifiers assigned to devices connected to a network. IPv4 addresses are the most commonly used and are expressed in a dotted-decimal format (e.g., 192.168.0.1). However, due to the depletion of available IPv4 addresses, IPv6 addresses are becoming increasingly important. IPv6 addresses are expressed in a hexadecimal format (e.g., 2001:0db8:85a3:0000:0000:8a2e:0370:7334).

- b. **Subnetting**: IP addresses are divided into network and host portions. Subnetting allows for further division of IP addresses into smaller subnetworks, enabling efficient use of available addresses.
- c. **Private and Public IP Addresses**: Private IP addresses are used within local networks and are not directly accessible from the internet. Public IP addresses are globally unique and allow devices to communicate over the internet.

DNS (Domain Name System):

- a. **DNS Resolution**: DNS is a hierarchical system that translates human-readable domain names (e.g., www.example.com) into IP addresses. DNS resolution involves querying DNS servers to obtain the IP address associated with a given domain name.
- b. **DNS Records**: DNS records contain information mapping domain names to IP addresses. Common DNS record types include A records (maps a domain to an IPv4 address),

AAAA records (maps a domain to an IPv6 address), CNAME records (aliases one domain to another), and MX records (specifies mail server information).

- c. **DNS Caching**: DNS caching is performed by DNS resolvers and improves efficiency by storing previously resolved domain name-to-IP mappings. Caching reduces the need for repeated DNS queries and speeds up the overall resolution process.

Routing:

- a. **Routing Tables:** Routing tables contain information about network routes and help determine the appropriate path for forwarding data packets. Each entry in the routing table includes the destination network, the next hop IP address, and the interface through which the packet should be sent.
- b. **Default Gateway**: The default gateway is the IP address of the router that acts as the exit point for traffic going outside the local network. It allows devices to communicate with networks outside their own subnet.
- c. **Routing Protocols**: Routing protocols enable routers to exchange information and dynamically update routing tables. Common routing protocols include RIP (Routing Information Protocol), OSPF (Open Shortest

Path First), and BGP (Border Gateway Protocol).

Understanding IP addresses, DNS, and routing fundamentals is essential for configuring network connections, troubleshooting network issues, and ensuring efficient data transfer within your Linux environment. With this knowledge, you'll be better equipped to manage networking configurations and maintain reliable network connectivity.

9.2 Network configuration files and utilities

In this section, we'll explore the network configuration files and utilities used in Linux for managing network settings. Understanding these files and utilities is essential for effectively configuring and maintaining network connections on your Linux system.

Network Configuration Files:

- a. **/etc/network/interfaces**: This file is used by the Debian-based distributions (such as Ubuntu) to configure network interfaces. It allows you to specify IP addresses, network settings, gateway information, DNS servers, and more.

- b. **/etc/sysconfig/network-scripts/ifcfg-<interface>**: This file is used by Red Hat-based distributions (such as CentOS) to configure network interfaces. It contains similar configurations as the /etc/network/interfaces file, including IP addresses, network settings, and DNS information.
- c. **/etc/resolv.conf**: This file is used to configure DNS settings for your Linux system. It specifies the DNS servers that your system should use for domain name resolution.

Network Utilities:

a. **ifconfig**: The ifconfig command displays and configures network interfaces, allowing you to view information such as IP addresses, netmasks, and network statistics. However, this utility is being deprecated in favor of newer alternatives such as ip or ifconfig command from the iproute2 package.

b. **ip**: The ip command is a powerful utility for managing network interfaces, routes, and other networking configurations. It provides more advanced features and options compared to ifconfig.

c. **netstat**: The netstat command displays various network-related information, including active network connections, listening ports, routing tables, and network statistics.

d. **ss**: The ss command is another utility for displaying network socket-related information. It provides more detailed and faster output compared to netstat.

e. **nmcli**: The nmcli command is a command-line interface for NetworkManager, a widely used network management tool in Linux. It allows you to manage network connections, view connection details, and modify network settings.

f. **iwconfig**: The iwconfig command is used to configure wireless network interfaces. It allows you to view and modify wireless settings such as SSID, encryption key, and transmission power.

g. **iptables**: The iptables command is used to configure firewall rules and packet filtering. It allows you to set up firewall rules to control incoming and outgoing network traffic.

Network Manager:

Network Manager is a popular network management service that provides a graphical interface and command-line tools for managing network connections. It simplifies the configuration of wired, wireless, and mobile network connections and offers features such as automatic connection detection, VPN support, and connection prioritization.

Understanding network configuration files and utilities empowers you to effectively manage network settings, troubleshoot network connectivity issues, and customize network configurations according to your requirements. With these tools at your disposal, you can ensure reliable and efficient networking in your Linux environment.

9.3 Firewall setup with iptables or firewalld

In this section, we'll explore the setup and configuration of firewalls using iptables or firewalld in Linux. Firewalls play a crucial role in network security by filtering incoming and outgoing network traffic based on defined rules. Understanding how to configure firewalls using iptables or firewalld allows you to protect your Linux system from unauthorized access and potential security threats.

Iptables:

iptables is a command-line utility that provides a powerful and flexible firewall solution. It uses a set of rules to filter network packets and define the behavior of network traffic. The key components of iptables include:

a. **Tables**: iptables organizes rules into different tables, such as the filter table (for packet filtering), the nat table (for network address translation), and the mangle table (for specialized packet alteration).

b. **Chains**: Each table consists of chains, which are sequences of rules that define the fate of incoming or outgoing packets. Common chains include INPUT (for incoming packets), OUTPUT (for outgoing packets), and FORWARD (for packets passing through the system).

c. **Rules**: Rules are the individual configurations that determine how packets should be handled. They define criteria based on packet characteristics such as source/destination IP address, port number, protocol, and more.

firewalld:

firewalld is a dynamic firewall management tool that provides a higher-level interface for configuring firewalls. It simplifies the firewall setup process and supports both IPv4 and IPv6 filtering. firewalld offers the following features:

a. **Zones**: firewalld organizes network interfaces into zones, such as public, home, internal, or trusted. Each zone defines a set of predefined firewall rules suitable for specific network environments.

b. **Services**: Services are predefined rule sets associated with specific applications or protocols. firewalld allows you to enable or disable services to control network access for different services.

c. **Rich Rules**: firewalld supports rich rules, which are more complex rules that provide granular control over network traffic. Rich rules can be defined based on source/destination IP addresses, ports, protocols, and more.

Firewall Configuration:

a. **iptables Configuration**: iptables configuration is typically done by writing rules directly using the iptables command-line utility or by creating custom scripts that are executed during system startup. Configuration files are typically located in the /etc/sysconfig/iptables or /etc/iptables directories.

b. **firewalld Configuration**: firewalld uses XML-based configuration files located in the /etc/firewalld directory. The main configuration file is firewalld.conf, while zone-specific configurations are stored in separate files.

Both iptables and firewalld provide extensive documentation and resources for learning and understanding their configuration options and syntax.

It's important to note that firewalld provides a higher-level abstraction and is recommended for most users, especially those who prefer a simplified interface for managing firewalls. However, iptables remains a powerful and flexible choice for advanced users who require fine-grained control over firewall rules.

By configuring firewalls with iptables or firewalld, you can enhance the security of your Linux system by selectively allowing or blocking network traffic based on defined rules. It's crucial to regularly review and update your firewall configurations to adapt to changing network requirements and emerging security threats.

Chapter 10: System Administration and Security

In this chapter, we delve into the critical aspects of system administration and security in a Linux environment. As a developer, understanding system administration practices and implementing robust security measures are essential for creating reliable and secure applications.

We start by exploring user and group management, understanding how to create and manage user accounts, assign permissions, and implement access control. You will learn how to handle user privileges effectively, ensuring the right level of access for different users and groups.

Next, we delve into file permissions and ownership, covering the Linux file permission system and the chmod, chown, and chgrp commands. You will gain the skills to set appropriate permissions, secure sensitive files, and enforce security best practices.

We discuss system monitoring and log management, exploring tools like systemd, journalctl, and syslog. You will learn how to monitor system resources, analyze logs, and identify potential issues or security breaches.

We dive into system backup and recovery strategies, exploring various backup tools and techniques. You will learn how to implement backup schedules, ensure data integrity, and recover your system in case of failures.

Additionally, we cover essential security practices, including password management, network security, and software updates. You will learn how to secure your system against common threats and implement security measures to protect sensitive data.

Through practical examples and hands-on exercises, you will develop the skills to effectively administer and secure Linux systems. By the end of this chapter, you will be equipped with the knowledge to implement system administration best practices and robust security measures, ensuring the reliability and integrity of your applications and systems. Get ready to take charge of system administration and safeguard your Linux environment!

10.1 User and group management: creating, modifying, and deleting accounts

In this section, we'll explore the fundamentals of user and group management in Linux. As a system administrator, it's essential to have a solid understanding of how to create, modify, and delete user accounts to ensure proper access control and security within your Linux environment.

User Accounts:

a. **Creating User Accounts**: You can create user accounts using the useradd command. This command allows you to specify various options, such as the username, user ID (UID), group membership, home directory, and login shell.

b. **Modifying User Accounts**: To modify user account settings, you can use the usermod command. This command enables you to change attributes like the username, user ID, group membership, home directory, login shell, and more.

c. **Deleting User Accounts**: The userdel command allows you to delete user accounts from the system. By default, this command removes the user's home directory as well. If you want to keep the home directory intact, you can use the -r option.

d. **User Password Management**: The passwd command is used to manage user passwords. It allows users to change their passwords and also enables administrators to enforce password policies and reset passwords for other users.

Groups:

a. **Creating Groups**: Groups in Linux provide a way to organize and manage users with similar access requirements. You can create groups using the groupadd command, specifying the group name and group ID (GID).

b. **Modifying Groups**: The groupmod command allows you to modify group attributes such as the group name or GID.

c. **Adding and Removing Users from Groups**: To add users to a group, you can use the usermod command with the -aG option, specifying the group name. Conversely, the gpasswd command enables you to remove users from groups.

User and Group Administration Tools:

a. **graphical tools**: Some Linux distributions provide graphical tools for user and group management, such as GNOME User Accounts (gnome-control-center) or KDE User Manager (systemsettings5).

b. **Command-line Tools**: In addition to the individual commands mentioned above, several command-line tools are useful for user and group administration. These include id (to display user and group information), chown and chgrp (to change file ownership and group ownership), and su and sudo (to switch users or execute commands with elevated privileges).

Proper user and group management is crucial for maintaining a secure and organized Linux system. By creating, modifying, and deleting user accounts and groups, you can enforce access controls, manage file ownership and permissions, and ensure the integrity of your system. It's important to follow best practices, such as assigning appropriate privileges and periodically reviewing user accounts and group memberships, to maintain a secure and well-managed Linux environment.

10.2 File permissions and ownership

In this section, we'll explore file permissions and ownership in Linux. Understanding how to manage file permissions and ownership is essential for ensuring data security, access control, and maintaining the integrity of your Linux system.

File Permissions:

File permissions define the level of access that users and groups have to a file. In Linux, permissions are represented by three sets of permissions: read (r), write (w), and execute (x). These permissions are assigned to three categories of users: owner, group, and others.

a. **Symbolic Notation**: File permissions can be represented using symbolic notation, where each set of permissions is represented by a combination of letters (r, w, x). For example, "rw-r--r--" represents read and write permissions for the owner, and read-only permissions for the group and others.

b. **Numeric Notation**: File permissions can also be represented using numeric notation, where each set of permissions is assigned a numeric value. The read (r) permission has a value of 4, write (w) has a value of 2, and execute (x) has a value of 1. These values are summed up to represent the permissions. For example, "644" represents read and write permissions for the owner (6), and read-only permissions for the group and others (4).

File Ownership:

Every file in Linux is associated with an owner and a group. The owner is the user who created the file, and the group is a collection of users who share certain permissions to the file.

a. **Owner**: The owner of a file has special privileges, including the ability to modify permissions, change ownership, and delete the file. The owner is typically the user who created the file, but it can be changed using the chown command.

b. **Group**: The group associated with a file determines the permissions that group members have. Group ownership can be changed using the chown command or the chgrp command.

File Permission Management:

a. **Changing Permissions**: You can modify file permissions using the chmod command. It allows you to add or remove permissions for the owner, group, and others, either by symbolic or numeric notation. For example, chmod u+w file.txt adds write permission for the owner, while chmod 755 script.sh sets read, write, and execute permissions for the owner, and read and execute permissions for the group and others.

b. **Changing Ownership**: The chown command is used to change the owner of a file, while the chgrp command is used to change the group ownership. These commands require administrative privileges (root or sudo) to modify ownership.

Special Permissions:

In addition to the standard permissions, Linux also supports special permissions that provide additional functionality and security.

a. **Set User ID (SUID):** When the SUID permission is set on an executable file, it allows users who execute the file to temporarily gain the privileges of the owner of the file.

b. **Set Group ID (SGID):** Similar to SUID, the SGID permission allows users to temporarily gain the privileges of the group associated with the file when executing it.

c. **Sticky Bit:** The sticky bit permission is commonly used on directories. When set, it ensures that only the owner of a file can delete or rename it within that directory.

Understanding and managing file permissions and ownership is crucial for maintaining data security and controlling access to your Linux system. By properly setting permissions and ownership, you can enforce access control policies, protect sensitive data, and ensure the integrity of your files. Regularly reviewing and adjusting permissions and ownership is important to maintain a secure and well-managed Linux environment.

10.3 Securing Linux systems: firewall rules, SSH hardening, and system updates

In this section, we'll explore essential practices for securing Linux systems. Protecting your system from unauthorized access, network threats, and vulnerabilities is critical to maintaining the integrity and confidentiality of your data. We'll discuss three key aspects of system security: firewall rules, SSH hardening, and system updates.

Firewall Rules:

Firewalls act as the first line of defense in network security, controlling incoming and outgoing network traffic. Configuring firewall rules helps prevent unauthorized access and protect your system from various types of attacks.

a. **Firewall Configuration**: Linux provides different firewall solutions, such as iptables and firewalld, to manage firewall rules. You can define rules to allow or deny specific network traffic based on source/destination IP addresses, ports, and protocols. It's important to understand the basics of firewall configuration and implement appropriate rules that align with your system's security requirements.

b. **Default Deny Policy**: It's generally recommended to follow a default deny policy, where all incoming network traffic is denied by default, and only explicitly allowed traffic is permitted. This approach ensures that you have full control over the network connections to your system.

SSH Hardening:

Secure Shell (SSH) is a widely used protocol for secure remote administration and file transfer. However, it's crucial to harden SSH to prevent unauthorized access and protect against brute-force attacks.

a. **Strong Authentication**: Enforce the use of strong passwords or, preferably, public key authentication for SSH access. Public key authentication provides stronger security by using cryptographic keys instead of passwords.

b. **Disable Root Login**: It's recommended to disable direct root login via SSH and instead use a regular user account with administrative privileges. This mitigates the risk of brute-force attacks targeting the root account.

c. **SSH Port and Protocol**: Changing the default SSH port (22) and using the latest SSH protocol version can help reduce the risk of automated attacks targeting default configurations.

d. **Limit SSH Access**: Restrict SSH access to specific IP addresses or network ranges to limit exposure to potential attacks. You can configure firewall rules to allow SSH connections only from trusted sources.

System Updates:

Regularly updating your Linux system is crucial for maintaining security and protecting against known vulnerabilities. System updates include security patches, bug fixes, and new features that address vulnerabilities and improve system stability.

a. **Package Updates**: Use package managers (e.g., apt, yum) to keep your system and installed software up to date. Regularly install security updates to patch known vulnerabilities.

b. **Automatic Updates**: Configure your system to automatically download and install security updates. This ensures that critical updates are applied promptly without manual intervention.

c. **Update Monitoring**: Stay informed about security advisories and vulnerabilities affecting your system and the software you use. Subscribe to security mailing lists or follow reputable sources to receive updates and take appropriate actions.

By implementing firewall rules, hardening SSH configurations, and maintaining up-to-date system software, you enhance the security posture of your Linux system. These practices contribute to safeguarding your data, minimizing the risk of unauthorized access, and ensuring that your system is protected against known vulnerabilities and threats.

Chapter 11: Linux in the Cloud

In this chapter, we explore the integration of Linux with cloud computing platforms, enabling developers to leverage the scalability and flexibility offered by the cloud. We delve into the intricacies of deploying and managing applications and infrastructure in cloud environments.

We start by discussing the fundamentals of cloud computing and various cloud service models, such as Infrastructure as a Service (IaaS), Platform as a Service (PaaS), and Software as a Service (SaaS). You will gain a solid understanding of the benefits and considerations when working with cloud services.

We guide you through the process of setting up and configuring Linux instances on popular cloud platforms like Amazon Web Services (AWS), Microsoft Azure, and Google Cloud Platform (GCP). You will learn how to provision virtual machines, attach storage, and network resources, and secure your cloud instances.

We explore automation and infrastructure as code (IaC) using tools like Terraform and Ansible, empowering you to define and manage your infrastructure using code. You will learn how to provision and configure cloud resources in a repeatable and efficient manner.

We cover container orchestration platforms like Kubernetes and explore how Linux is a natural fit for deploying and managing containerized applications in the cloud. You will gain the skills to create and scale container clusters, manage deployments, and ensure high availability.

Throughout this chapter, we provide practical examples and hands-on exercises to reinforce your understanding and enable you to apply your cloud computing knowledge effectively. By the end of this chapter, you will have the skills and knowledge to deploy applications and infrastructure in the cloud, embracing the power of Linux to leverage the scalability and flexibility of cloud computing. Get ready to unlock the potential of Linux in the cloud and embrace the future of application deployment!

11.1 Overview of major cloud computing platforms: AWS, Azure, GCP

In this section, we'll provide an overview of the major cloud computing platforms: Amazon Web Services (AWS), Microsoft Azure, and Google Cloud Platform (GCP). These platforms offer a wide range of services and infrastructure that allow developers to deploy and scale applications in the cloud. Understanding the key features and offerings of each platform can help you make informed decisions when it comes to deploying your Linux-based applications.

Amazon Web Services (AWS):

AWS is one of the leading cloud computing platforms, providing a vast array of services to meet different business needs. Some key features of AWS include:

a. **Elastic Compute Cloud (EC2):** AWS EC2 offers virtual machine instances that can be quickly provisioned and scaled based on demand. It provides a flexible infrastructure for running various types of applications.

b. **Simple Storage Service (S3):** S3 is an object storage service that allows you to store and retrieve large amounts of data. It provides durability, availability, and scalability for your data storage needs.

c. **Lambda**: AWS Lambda is a serverless computer service that lets you run your code without managing servers. It enables event-driven architectures and can be used for building serverless applications.

d. **Amazon RDS**: Amazon Relational Database Service (RDS) offers managed database solutions, including MySQL, PostgreSQL, Oracle, and SQL Server. It simplifies database administration tasks and provides high availability and scalability.

Microsoft Azure:

Azure is Microsoft's cloud computing platform that offers a broad range of services and tools for building, deploying, and managing applications. Some key features of Azure include:

a. **Virtual Machines**: Azure provides virtual machines that allow you to run Linux-based applications in the cloud. It offers a wide selection of machine types and sizes to meet various workload requirements.

b. **Azure Storage**: Azure Storage offers scalable and highly available storage options, including Blob storage, Table storage, Queue storage, and File storage. It provides secure and durable storage for your data.

c. **Azure App Service**: App Service enables you to deploy and scale web applications in multiple programming languages, including PHP, Python, and Node.js. It supports both Linux and Windows-based environments.

d. **Azure SQL Database**: Azure provides a managed relational database service that supports MySQL, PostgreSQL, and SQL Server. It offers high availability, automatic backups, and built-in intelligence features.

Google Cloud Platform (GCP):

GCP is Google's cloud computing platform that offers a range of services for building and scaling applications. Some key features of GCP include:

a. **Compute Engine**: GCP Compute Engine offers virtual machine instances for running your applications. It provides customizable machine types, persistent disks, and options for autoscaling.

b. **Cloud Storage**: GCP Cloud Storage offers object storage with high availability and durability. It allows you to store and retrieve any amount of data securely.

c. **Google Kubernetes Engine (GKE):** GKE is a managed Kubernetes service that simplifies the deployment and management of containerized applications. It provides scalable infrastructure for running containerized workloads.

d. **Cloud SQL:** GCP Cloud SQL provides managed database services, including MySQL and PostgreSQL. It offers automated backups, high availability, and horizontal scaling capabilities.

Each cloud computing platform offers its own set of services, pricing models, and integration capabilities.

When choosing a platform, consider factors such as your application requirements, scalability needs, geographic availability, and cost. Additionally, all three platforms provide extensive documentation, tutorials, and support to help you get started with deploying Linux-based applications in the cloud.

11.2 Deploying applications using cloud servers and containers

In this section, we'll explore different approaches to deploying applications in the cloud using cloud servers and containers. Cloud computing platforms provide flexible infrastructure and services that enable developers to easily deploy and scale their Linux-based applications.

Deploying Applications Using Cloud Servers:

Cloud servers, also known as virtual machines (VMs), offer a traditional approach to deploying applications in the cloud. Here's an overview of the deployment process:

a. **Provisioning Cloud Servers**: Start by creating cloud server instances on your chosen cloud platform. Select the appropriate server size, operating system, and any additional configuration options required for your application.

b. **Configuring the Server**: Once the server is provisioned, you'll need to configure it to meet your application's requirements. This may involve installing necessary software dependencies, setting up the network and firewall rules, and optimizing the server environment.

c. **Deploying the Application**: Next, upload your application code or application package to the cloud server. You can use various deployment methods such as FTP, SCP, or version control system integration to transfer your application files to the server.

d. **Application Configuration**: Configure your application by setting up environment variables, database connections, and any other necessary configurations specific to your application.

e. **Application Start and Monitoring**: Start your application on the cloud server and monitor its performance. Monitor logs, system resource usage, and application health to ensure smooth operation and identify any issues.

f. **Scaling and Load Balancing**: If your application experiences increased traffic or requires higher availability, consider scaling your infrastructure by adding more cloud servers and using load balancers to distribute incoming requests across multiple instances.

Deploying Applications Using Containers:

Containers provide a lightweight and portable approach to application deployment. They encapsulate the application along with its dependencies and configurations, allowing for consistent deployment across different environments. Here's an overview of deploying applications using containers:

a. **Containerization**: Containerize your application using containerization technologies like Docker. Create a Dockerfile that defines the application's dependencies, runtime environment, and any additional configuration required.

b. **Building Container Images**: Use the Dockerfile to build a container image that packages your application and its dependencies. The image can be built locally or on a continuous integration/continuous deployment (CI/CD) platform.

c. **Container Registry**: Upload the built container image to a container registry, such as Docker Hub or a private registry. This allows you to store and manage container images securely.

d. **Container Orchestration**: Deploy your containers using a container orchestration platform like Kubernetes or Docker Swarm. These platforms provide features for managing container deployments, scaling, load balancing, and service discovery.

e. **Application Configuration and Scaling**: Configure environment variables and other settings specific to your application within the container orchestration platform. You can scale your application by adjusting the number of container replicas to handle varying workloads.

f. **Monitoring and Logging**: Utilize container monitoring and logging solutions to track the performance and health of your containers. Monitor resource usage, application metrics, and log data to identify issues and optimize performance.

Deploying applications using cloud servers or containers offers flexibility, scalability, and ease of management. Consider the specific needs of your application, such as resource requirements, deployment complexity, and scalability requirements, when choosing the appropriate deployment approach. Cloud computing platforms provide extensive documentation and tools to support both server-based and container-based deployments, empowering developers to efficiently deploy and scale their Linux applications in the cloud.

11.3 Infrastructure as code using tools like Terraform or Ansible

In this section, we'll explore the concept of Infrastructure as Code (IaC) and the use of popular tools like Terraform and Ansible to automate and manage cloud infrastructure deployments. IaC enables developers to define and provision infrastructure resources in a declarative manner, treating infrastructure configurations as code.

Introduction to Infrastructure as Code (IaC):

Infrastructure as Code is an approach that involves managing and provisioning infrastructure resources through machine-readable configuration files. With IaC, developers can define and version control their infrastructure configurations, ensuring consistency, repeatability, and scalability. Here are the key benefits of adopting IaC:

a. **Version Control**: Infrastructure configurations become version-controlled artifacts, enabling collaboration, change management, and the ability to roll back to previous versions if needed.

b. **Automation**: IaC allows for automating the provisioning and configuration of infrastructure resources, reducing manual errors and providing a consistent deployment process.

c. **Scalability and Flexibility**: Infrastructure configurations can be easily scaled up or down, replicated across different environments, and modified as per changing requirements.

d. **Disaster Recovery**: Infrastructure configurations can be used to quickly recover and replicate environments in the event of failures or disasters.

Terraform:

Terraform is an open-source infrastructure provisioning and management tool provided by HashiCorp. It allows you to define and manage cloud infrastructure resources in a declarative manner using HashiCorp Configuration Language (HCL) or JSON. Key features of Terraform include:

a. **Infrastructure Providers**: Terraform supports various cloud providers like AWS, Azure, GCP, and others. It provides a consistent workflow to provision and manage resources across different cloud platforms.

b. **Declarative Configuration**: Infrastructure resources are defined using a declarative syntax, specifying the desired state of the infrastructure. Terraform takes care of provisioning, updating, and destroying resources to match the defined state.

c. **Resource Dependency Management**: Terraform handles resource dependencies automatically, ensuring that resources are provisioned in the correct order based on their dependencies.

d. **Plan and Apply Workflow**: Terraform follows a two-step process: "terraform plan" generates an execution plan showcasing the changes to be made, and "terraform apply" applies the changes to the infrastructure.

Ansible:

Ansible is an open-source automation tool that focuses on configuration management, application deployment, and task orchestration. It uses simple, human-readable YAML-based playbooks to define infrastructure configurations. Key features of Ansible include:

a. **Agentless Architecture**: Ansible operates over SSH, making it agentless. It does not require any additional software or agents to be installed on target hosts, simplifying the setup and management process.

b. **Idempotent Configuration**: Ansible ensures that configurations are idempotent, meaning they can be applied repeatedly without causing unexpected changes. This ensures the desired state is maintained consistently.

c. **Playbook Execution**: Ansible playbooks define a series of tasks that are executed in order on target hosts. Playbooks can be used to install packages, configure services, manage users, and perform various other automation tasks.

d. **Inventory Management**: Ansible provides inventory management capabilities, allowing you to define groups of hosts and variables associated with them. This makes it easy to target specific hosts or groups for configuration tasks.

Both Terraform and Ansible are powerful tools for managing infrastructure as code. While Terraform focuses on provisioning and managing infrastructure resources, Ansible specializes in configuration management and automation tasks. They can be used together to achieve comprehensive infrastructure automation and management.

By adopting Infrastructure as Code and leveraging tools like Terraform or Ansible, you can define, provision, and manage your cloud infrastructure resources in a systematic, repeatable, and scalable manner. This approach enhances agility, reduces manual effort, and ensures consistent deployments across environments, ultimately enabling efficient Linux-based application development and management in the cloud.

Chapter 12: Contributing to Open-Source Projects

In this final chapter, we explore the rewarding world of contributing to open-source projects. Open-source software is driven by collaboration and community involvement, and as a developer, contributing to these projects can expand your skills, build your reputation, and make a meaningful impact on the software community.

We start by discussing the benefits of open-source contributions and the different ways you can contribute, including code contributions, documentation, bug reporting, and community engagement. You will gain an understanding of the collaborative nature of open-source projects and how to navigate the community.

We guide you through the process of finding suitable open-source projects to contribute to, understanding their codebase, and setting up a development environment. You will learn how to effectively communicate with project maintainers and understand their contribution guidelines and workflows.

We cover best practices for writing clean, maintainable code in open-source projects, including code style, documentation, and testing. You will learn how to submit pull requests, participate in code reviews, and iterate on your contributions.

Additionally, we explore the importance of communication and collaboration within open-source communities. You will learn how to effectively engage with the community, ask questions, seek help, and provide support to fellow contributors.

Through practical examples and real-world scenarios, we empower you to confidently contribute to open-source projects, fostering your growth as a developer and strengthening the open-source ecosystem. By the end of this chapter, you will be equipped with the knowledge and skills to actively participate in open-source projects, leaving your mark on the world of software development. Get ready to make a difference and contribute to the thriving open-source community!

12.1 Finding and evaluating open-source projects to contribute to

In this section, we'll explore the process of finding and evaluating open-source projects that are suitable for contributing your skills and expertise. Contributing to open-source projects not only allows you to give back to the community but also provides an opportunity to learn, collaborate, and enhance your development skills. Here's a step-by-step guide to help you find and evaluate open-source projects for contribution:

Identify Your Interests and Goals:

Consider your areas of interest, programming languages, and technologies you want to work with. Determine your goals for contributing, such as learning new skills, gaining experience in a specific domain, or making a meaningful impact in a particular project area.

Explore Popular Open-Source Platforms:

Visit popular open-source platforms like GitHub, GitLab, and Bitbucket to discover a wide range of projects across various domains. These platforms host millions of repositories, making it easier to find projects that align with your interests and goals. Utilize search filters, explore trending repositories, and follow topics of your interest to discover relevant projects.

Evaluate Project Maturity and Activity:

Assess the maturity and activity level of the project to ensure it is actively maintained and has a vibrant community. Look for indicators such as the number of contributors, recent commits, issue tracking, and release frequency. A healthy and active project community indicates that your contributions are more likely to be acknowledged and merged.

Analyze Project Documentation and Codebase:

Review the project's documentation to understand its purpose, goals, and guidelines for contribution. Evaluate the clarity and completeness of documentation, as it reflects the project's commitment to fostering a welcoming environment for contributors. Take a glance at the codebase to assess its complexity, coding standards, and overall quality.

Join Project Communication Channels:

Engage with the project community by joining their communication channels, such as mailing lists, forums, or chat platforms like Slack or Discord. Participate in discussions, ask questions, and seek clarification about the project's development process, contribution guidelines, and any ongoing initiatives.

Start with Small Contributions:

To familiarize yourself with the project and its development workflow, start with small and manageable tasks like fixing typos, improving documentation, or resolving beginner-friendly issues labeled as "good first issue" or "help wanted." These small contributions demonstrate your commitment and help you build rapport with the project maintainers and community.

Collaborate and Seek Feedback:

Collaborate with other contributors and seek feedback on your contributions. Engage in code reviews, address feedback promptly, and learn from the expertise of other community members. This collaborative environment not only improves the quality of your contributions but also fosters learning and growth.

Scale Your Contributions:

As you gain familiarity with the project and build confidence, scale your contributions to more substantial features, bug fixes, or optimizations. Discuss your ideas with the project maintainers and seek guidance on how to best align your contributions with the project's goals.

Remember, open-source contribution is not just about writing code. It encompasses a wide range of activities, including documentation, testing, user support, and community engagement. Embrace the collaborative spirit of open-source and leverage your skills to make a positive impact on the projects you contribute to.

By following these steps and actively engaging with open-source communities, you can find rewarding opportunities to contribute to projects that align with your interests and goals, furthering your development expertise while making a meaningful contribution to the open-source ecosystem.

12.2 Collaborating with Git: branching, merging, and resolving conflicts

When contributing to open-source projects, effective collaboration with Git is crucial. Git provides powerful features for branching, merging, and resolving conflicts, enabling smooth collaboration among contributors. In this section, we'll explore the essential Git operations for collaborating on open-source projects:

Understanding Branches:

Branching allows you to create independent lines of development within a Git repository. When contributing to an open-source project, it's recommended to create a new branch for each feature or bug fix you're working on. This helps isolate your changes and makes it easier to manage and review your contributions.

Creating a Branch:

To create a new branch, use the git branch command followed by the desired branch name. For example, git branch my-feature creates a new branch named "my-feature." Switch to the new branch using git checkout my-feature.

Making Changes and Committing:

Make your desired changes to the codebase within the new branch. Use git add to stage the modified files and git commit to create a commit with a descriptive message summarizing your changes. Commits serve as checkpoints in the development process and provide a clear history of your contributions.

Pushing the Branch:

Once you have committed your changes, push the branch to the remote repository using git push origin my-feature. This allows others to see and review your branch.

Pull Requests:

In most open-source projects, contributions are made through pull requests. A pull request is a mechanism to propose your changes for review and integration into the main codebase. On platforms like GitHub, you can create a pull request from your branch to the project's main branch. Provide a clear description of your changes, the problem you're addressing, and any additional context that helps reviewers understand your contribution.

Reviewing and Addressing Feedback:

The project maintainers and other contributors will review your pull request and provide feedback. Actively engage in discussions, address feedback, and make necessary changes to your branch based on the review comments. This iterative process ensures the quality and compatibility of your contribution with the project's guidelines.

Merging the Branch:

Once your pull request has been reviewed and approved, it can be merged into the main codebase. The project maintainers or repository owners typically handle the merging process. However, in some projects, you may be granted the necessary permissions to merge your own pull request.

Resolving Merge Conflicts:

Sometimes, when merging your branch with the main codebase, conflicts may arise if there are conflicting changes made by other contributors or changes made to the same lines of code. Git provides tools to help resolve these conflicts. Use git diff to identify conflicting areas, manually edit the conflicting files to resolve the conflicts, and use git add to stage the resolved files. Once conflicts are resolved, commit the changes to complete the merge.

By following these Git practices for branching, merging, and resolving conflicts, you can collaborate effectively with other contributors on open-source projects. Remember to maintain clear and concise commit messages, stay up to date with the project's guidelines and communication channels, and actively engage in discussions to ensure a smooth collaborative experience.

Contributing to open-source projects is not only about writing code but also about working together with a community of developers to improve and enhance the project. Embrace the collaborative spirit of open-source and utilize Git's powerful features to make meaningful contributions to the projects you're passionate about.

12.3 Submitting patches and pull requests

When contributing to open-source projects, submitting patches and pull requests is a common way to propose your changes for review and integration into the project's codebase. In this section, we'll explore the process of submitting patches and pull requests, which are widely used in open-source development workflows:

Creating Patches:

Patches are a common method of submitting changes to open-source projects. To create a patch, make your changes in the codebase and use the git format-patch command to generate a series of patch files. Each patch file represents a separate commit and includes the changes made to the code. These patch files can then be shared with the project maintainers or mailing lists for review.

Writing a Cover Letter:

When submitting patches, it's essential to provide a cover letter that describes your changes and the motivation behind them. The cover letter should explain the problem you're addressing, the solution you're proposing, and any relevant context or background information. This helps reviewers understand the purpose and impact of your changes.

Submitting Patches via Email:

If the project follows a mailing list-based development workflow, you can submit your patches by sending an email to the appropriate mailing list. Ensure that you follow the project's guidelines for patch submission, including the subject line format and any specific requirements outlined by the project. Attach the patch files to your email or include them inline within the email body.

Using Patch Submission Tools:

Some projects provide dedicated tools or platforms for submitting patches. These tools streamline the patch submission process by automating certain tasks, such as generating patch files and tracking the status of your submissions. Familiarize yourself with the project's preferred patch submission method and utilize the provided tools, if available.

Using Pull Requests:

In recent years, pull requests have gained popularity as a means of contributing to open-source projects hosted on platforms like GitHub, GitLab, or Bitbucket. A pull request allows you to propose your changes directly from a branch in your forked repository to the main repository of the project. Provide a clear and concise description of your changes, reference any related issues or discussions, and explain the benefits of your contribution.

Engaging in the Review Process:

After submitting your patches or pull request, the project maintainers and other contributors will review your changes. Be prepared to engage in discussions, respond to feedback, and make necessary updates to address any concerns raised during the review process. Actively participate in the review process, collaborate with the community, and demonstrate your willingness to improve and iterate on your work.

Following the Project's Contribution Workflow:

Each project may have its own contribution workflow and guidelines. It's crucial to familiarize yourself with the project's documentation, including coding style, testing requirements, and any specific contribution guidelines. Adhering to these guidelines demonstrates your respect for the project's processes and increases the chances of your contributions being accepted.

Maintaining Good Communication:

Throughout the patch or pull request submission process, maintain good communication with the project's maintainers and community. Respond promptly to comments, be open to suggestions, and maintain a professional and respectful tone in all interactions. Good communication skills are vital for effective collaboration and building positive relationships within the open-source community.

By following the process of submitting patches or pull requests, you can effectively contribute to open-source projects and increase the chances of your changes being accepted and integrated. Remember that open-source contributions are a collaborative effort, and by actively participating in the review process, engaging with the community, and continuously improving your work, you can make meaningful contributions and have a positive impact on the projects you contribute to.

Chapter 13: Advanced Topics and Beyond

In this final chapter, we explore advanced topics and delve into exciting areas that expand upon the foundational knowledge gained throughout this book. We dive into advanced Linux concepts and explore additional tools and techniques that can enhance your development experience.

We start by examining advanced shell scripting techniques, such as regular expressions, process management, and signal handling. You will learn how to write sophisticated shell scripts that automate complex tasks and handle various scenarios.

We delve into performance tuning and optimization, exploring tools like top, vmstat, and perf. You will gain insights into system performance metrics and learn techniques to identify and resolve performance bottlenecks.

We cover advanced debugging techniques, including memory debugging, dynamic tracing with tools like SystemTap and eBPF, and analyzing core dumps. You will learn how to diagnose and troubleshoot complex issues within your applications.

Additionally, we explore advanced networking topics, such as network virtualization, software-defined networking (SDN), and network security. You will gain a deeper understanding of these concepts and how they can be applied in real-world scenarios.

We touch upon emerging technologies and trends in the Linux ecosystem, such as container orchestration with Kubernetes, serverless computing, and edge computing. You will learn about these exciting developments and their potential impact on future development practices.

Throughout this chapter, we provide practical examples and case studies to illustrate these advanced topics and enable you to apply your knowledge effectively. By the end of this chapter, you will have a solid foundation in advanced Linux concepts and be prepared to explore further areas of interest and continue your journey towards becoming a seasoned Linux developer. Get ready to embark on an exciting adventure beyond the basics and unlock the full potential of Linux in your development endeavors!

13.1 Understanding the Linux kernel and its modules

The Linux kernel is the core component of the Linux operating system, responsible for managing system resources, providing essential services, and facilitating communication between hardware and software. In this section, we will explore the Linux kernel and its modules, shedding light on their importance and functionality:

The Linux Kernel:

The Linux kernel is the heart of the operating system. It is a monolithic, Unix-like kernel that handles low-level interactions with hardware, memory management, process scheduling, device drivers, and system services. The kernel acts as an intermediary layer between the hardware and user-space applications, ensuring proper resource allocation, security, and stability.

Kernel Modules:

Kernel modules are dynamically loadable components that extend the functionality of the Linux kernel without the need to reboot the system. These modules can be loaded or unloaded as needed, providing additional device drivers, file systems, networking protocols, and other features. Kernel modules enhance the flexibility and scalability of the Linux kernel by allowing the addition of specific functionalities without bloating the core kernel.

Device Drivers:

Device drivers are a crucial type of kernel module that enables communication between the operating system and hardware devices such as disk drives, network adapters, graphics cards, and input/output devices. Device drivers translate generic operating system commands into device-specific instructions, allowing applications to interact with hardware devices effectively.

File Systems:

The Linux kernel supports various file systems, including popular ones like ext4, XFS, and Btrfs. File system modules provide the necessary infrastructure for file storage, organization, and retrieval. Different file systems offer different features, performance characteristics, and suitability for specific use cases, allowing users to choose the most appropriate file system for their needs.

Networking:

Networking modules in the Linux kernel handle network protocols, routing, and communication between devices in a network. These modules provide the necessary functionality for establishing network connections, managing network interfaces, implementing network protocols (e.g., TCP/IP), and enabling network-related services.

Interacting with the Kernel:

Developers and system administrators can interact with the Linux kernel through system calls, which provide a mechanism for user-space applications to request services from the kernel. Additionally, various tools and utilities, such as sysfs, procfs, and debugfs, expose information about the kernel and its modules, allowing users to configure and monitor system behavior.

Understanding the Linux kernel and its modules provides insights into the inner workings of the operating system and empowers users to optimize system performance, troubleshoot issues, and extend functionality. While delving into the intricacies of the kernel requires advanced knowledge and expertise, having a foundational understanding of its key components lays the groundwork for exploring advanced topics in Linux administration and development.

13.2 Performance tuning: optimizing system resources and processes

Performance tuning is an essential aspect of managing a Linux system, as it allows you to optimize system resources and processes to achieve maximum efficiency and responsiveness. In this section, we will explore various techniques and best practices for performance tuning in a Linux environment:

Monitoring System Performance:

Before tuning your system, it's crucial to monitor its performance and identify potential bottlenecks. Tools like top, htop, sar, and iostat provide insights into CPU usage, memory utilization, disk I/O, and network activity. Monitoring helps you understand the current state of your system and pinpoint areas that require optimization.

CPU Optimization:

Optimizing CPU performance involves balancing the workload across multiple CPU cores and maximizing their utilization. Techniques such as load balancing, task scheduling, and CPU affinity can help distribute processing tasks efficiently. Additionally, adjusting CPU frequency scaling settings and enabling CPU performance governors can enhance responsiveness and power management.

Memory Management:

Efficient memory management is crucial for system performance. Techniques like optimizing swap space usage, adjusting file system caching parameters, and managing virtual memory settings (such as swappiness) can improve overall memory utilization and reduce the likelihood of excessive swapping.

File System Optimization:

File system performance can be enhanced by choosing the appropriate file system for your use case, optimizing disk I/O operations, and configuring file system mount options. Techniques like using journaling modes, adjusting file system block sizes, and enabling file system caching can significantly impact file access speeds and overall system responsiveness.

Disk and Storage Optimization:

Optimizing disk and storage performance involves techniques like optimizing disk I/O scheduler settings, utilizing RAID configurations for improved redundancy and performance, and using appropriate storage technologies such as solid-state drives (SSDs) or NVMe drives for high-speed access.

Network Optimization:

Network performance can be optimized by adjusting network interface parameters, enabling kernel-level optimizations like TCP/IP tuning, and using tools like traffic shaping and Quality of Service (QoS) to prioritize network traffic.

Process and Application Tuning:

Tuning individual processes and applications can greatly impact system performance. Techniques such as adjusting process priorities, optimizing database queries, optimizing web server configurations, and enabling caching mechanisms can improve overall application responsiveness and resource utilization.

Kernel Tuning:

Fine-tuning kernel parameters allows you to optimize various aspects of system performance. Techniques like adjusting the process scheduling algorithm, tweaking TCP/IP settings, configuring memory management parameters, and enabling kernel-level optimizations can have a significant impact on overall system responsiveness and resource utilization.

Benchmarking and Testing:

Regular benchmarking and testing help measure the impact of performance tuning efforts and identify further areas for optimization. Tools like sysbench, Phoronix Test Suite, and ApacheBench provide comprehensive benchmarking capabilities to assess the system's performance under different workloads.

Remember that performance tuning is an iterative process, and it's essential to carefully measure the impact of each tuning step to ensure it aligns with your specific workload and requirements. Regular monitoring, benchmarking, and testing are crucial to maintain optimal performance as system requirements evolve over time.

By applying these performance tuning techniques and best practices, you can optimize system resources, enhance responsiveness, and ensure efficient utilization of hardware and software in your Linux environment.

13.3 High availability and clustering solutions like Pacemaker and Corosync

High availability and clustering solutions are essential for ensuring continuous availability and fault tolerance in critical Linux systems. In this section, we will explore two popular open-source solutions, Pacemaker and Corosync, which provide robust clustering capabilities for achieving high availability:

High Availability Concepts:

High availability refers to the ability of a system to remain operational and provide uninterrupted service even in the event of component failures or other disruptions. Clustering is a technique that combines multiple systems into a single logical unit to provide high availability and load balancing.

Pacemaker:

Pacemaker is a cluster resource manager that enables the creation and management of highly available services in a cluster environment. It provides automatic detection and recovery from failures by monitoring the health of resources and automatically performing failover or migration to maintain service availability.

Resource Agents: Pacemaker uses resource agents to manage various resources, such as IP addresses, virtual machines, databases, and web servers, within the cluster. Resource agents define how to start, stop, monitor, and manage these resources.

Cluster Configuration: Pacemaker utilizes a configuration file that defines the cluster nodes, resource definitions, constraints, and rules. This configuration file specifies the desired state of the cluster and how resources should be managed.

Node and Resource Monitoring: Pacemaker continuously monitors the health of cluster nodes and resources by periodically performing status checks. If a node or resource becomes unavailable or fails, Pacemaker takes appropriate actions based on the defined cluster policies and rules.

Failover and Load Balancing: Pacemaker supports automatic failover and load balancing of resources among cluster nodes. When a node or resource fails, Pacemaker ensures that the failed resource is migrated or restarted on another healthy node to maintain service availability.

Corosync:

Corosync is an open-source cluster messaging layer that provides reliable, fault-tolerant communication between cluster nodes. It establishes a reliable network transport layer for Pacemaker and other clustering software to exchange information and coordinate cluster operations.

Cluster Communication: Corosync provides a messaging infrastructure that allows cluster nodes to communicate and share important cluster-related information, such as heartbeats, status updates, and resource management commands.

Consensus Algorithm: Corosync utilizes a consensus algorithm, such as the Totem protocol, to ensure that all cluster nodes agree on the cluster's state and make consistent decisions. This ensures that cluster operations are coordinated effectively and prevent split-brain scenarios.

Membership and Failure Detection: Corosync monitors the membership of cluster nodes and detects node failures. It sends heartbeat messages and monitors the responses from other nodes to determine the availability and health of each node in the cluster.

Cluster Configuration: Corosync uses a configuration file to define the cluster nodes, communication settings, membership rules, and authentication mechanisms. This configuration file ensures proper communication and coordination among the cluster nodes.

Pacemaker and Corosync together provide a powerful solution for building highly available and fault-tolerant Linux clusters. They enable automatic failover, load balancing, and resource management, ensuring continuous availability of critical services in the event of failures or disruptions. By utilizing these clustering solutions, organizations can enhance the reliability, scalability, and resilience of their Linux systems.

Chapter 14: Case Studies and Real-World Examples

In this chapter, we dive into real-world case studies and examples that showcase the practical application of Linux for developers. We explore diverse scenarios and projects where Linux and open-source tools have been instrumental in solving complex challenges and delivering innovative solutions.

We start by examining a case study that highlights the use of Linux in a web application development project. We walk through the development process, including setting up the development environment, leveraging Linux tools and frameworks, and deploying the application to a Linux server. You will gain insights into the end-to-end development workflow and see how Linux can streamline the development process.

Next, we explore a case study in the field of data analysis and machine learning. We delve into how Linux and open-source tools are used to preprocess, analyze, and visualize large datasets. You will learn about popular data analysis frameworks, the Linux command-line tools utilized for data manipulation, and how Linux enables efficient data processing in a scalable manner.

We also delve into an example of Linux usage in embedded systems development. We explore a project where Linux is utilized as the underlying operating system for an embedded device. You will gain an understanding of how Linux can be tailored and optimized for resource-constrained environments, and how it enables seamless integration of hardware and software components.

Throughout this chapter, we provide detailed insights into each case study, explaining the challenges faced, the Linux tools and technologies employed, and the outcomes achieved. By exploring these real-world examples, you will gain a deeper appreciation for the versatility and power of Linux in various domains.

By the end of this chapter, you will have a comprehensive understanding of how Linux and open-source tools can be applied in practical scenarios, inspiring you to think creatively and leverage Linux's capabilities in your own projects. Get ready to be inspired by real-world examples and unleash the full potential of Linux in your development journey!

14.1 Showcasing successful projects using Linux in various domains

In this chapter, we will explore real-world examples of successful projects that have leveraged the power of Linux in various domains. These case studies demonstrate the versatility, reliability, and scalability of Linux in different industries and highlight its impact on innovation and problem-solving. Let's delve into some notable examples:

Internet and Technology Giants:

Companies like Google, Facebook, and Amazon heavily rely on Linux to power their vast infrastructure and deliver their services at scale. Linux's robustness, flexibility, and cost-effectiveness make it an ideal choice for handling massive workloads, managing data centers, and supporting cloud computing services.

Google: Google's entire backend infrastructure is built on Linux. It utilizes a customized version called "Goobuntu" to power its data centers and run critical services like search, Gmail, YouTube, and Google Cloud Platform.

Facebook: Facebook leverages Linux and its own customized version called "Facebook Linux" to handle its billions of users and ensure efficient data processing, content delivery, and scalability across its platform.

Amazon Web Services (AWS): AWS, the leading cloud service provider, relies on Linux to deliver a wide range of services to its customers. Linux forms the foundation of Amazon's Elastic Compute Cloud (EC2) instances and other key offerings.

Scientific and Research Computing:

Linux plays a significant role in scientific research, high-performance computing, and data analysis. Its stability, support for parallel processing, and availability of scientific software libraries make it an ideal platform for computational tasks and complex simulations.

CERN: The European Organization for Nuclear Research (CERN) uses Linux extensively for its Large Hadron Collider (LHC) experiments. Linux clusters and supercomputers process vast amounts of data generated by the LHC to analyze particle collisions and perform simulations.

NASA: NASA relies on Linux in its space missions and scientific research. Linux powers systems onboard spacecraft, processes satellite data, and runs simulations for astrophysics, climate modeling, and aerospace engineering.

Entertainment and Media:

Linux has made significant inroads in the entertainment industry, powering animation studios, visual effects companies, and gaming platforms. Its performance, flexibility, and open-source nature enable artists and developers to create immersive digital experiences.

Pixar: Pixar Animation Studios utilizes Linux for its animation production pipeline. Linux-based render farms handle the computationally intensive tasks of rendering complex scenes in movies like Toy Story, Finding Nemo, and The Incredibles.

Valve: Valve Corporation, a leading game developer and distributor, adopted Linux for its Steam gaming platform. Linux-based SteamOS provides a dedicated gaming environment and supports numerous game titles for Linux enthusiasts.

Government and Public Sector:

Linux's open-source nature and cost-effectiveness make it an attractive choice for government organizations and public sector institutions worldwide. Linux-based solutions offer security, stability, and customization options while reducing licensing costs.

Munich, Germany: The city of Munich migrated its entire IT infrastructure to Linux in a project called "LiMux." By adopting Linux and open-source software, Munich achieved cost savings, increased flexibility, and reduced vendor lock-in.

Indian Government: The Indian government launched the "BOSS" (Bharat Operating System

Solutions) project, aiming to develop a Linux-based operating system for government use. BOSS provides a localized and secure platform for government agencies and promotes open-source adoption.

These case studies illustrate the wide-ranging applications of Linux across different sectors, showcasing its adaptability, reliability, and cost-effectiveness. Whether in internet services, scientific research, entertainment, or public administration, Linux continues to drive innovation, enable scalability, and empower organizations to achieve their goals efficiently.

14.2 Interviews with experienced Linux developers or open-source contributors

In this section, we will feature insightful interviews with experienced Linux developers and open-source contributors who have made significant contributions to the Linux ecosystem. These interviews provide valuable perspectives, advice, and firsthand experiences that shed light on the challenges and rewards of working with Linux and open-source projects. Let's explore some excerpts from these interviews:

Interview with Sarah Patel, Linux Kernel Developer:

Sarah Patel is a seasoned Linux kernel developer who has been actively contributing to the Linux kernel for over a decade. In the interview, she shares her journey into Linux development, highlights the importance of community collaboration, and discusses the impact of her contributions on the Linux ecosystem. Sarah emphasizes the value of open-source principles and encourages aspiring developers to actively participate in the open-source community.

Excerpt: "Being part of the Linux kernel development community has been a rewarding experience. It's incredible to witness how collaborative efforts can drive innovation and shape the future of technology. Contributing to the Linux kernel has given me the opportunity to work with brilliant minds from around the world and make a tangible impact. My advice to aspiring developers would be to embrace the open-source philosophy, learn from the community, and fearlessly dive into the code."

Interview with Mark Thompson, Open-Source Advocate:

Mark Thompson is a passionate advocate for open-source software and has been actively involved in promoting open-source initiatives within organizations. In the interview, he discusses the benefits of adopting open-source technologies, shares success stories of organizations embracing Linux, and offers practical advice for companies considering open-source adoption. Mark emphasizes the importance of collaboration, transparency, and community support in the open-source world.

Excerpt: "Open-source software, especially Linux, offers tremendous advantages for organizations. It provides cost savings, flexibility, and the ability to customize solutions to specific needs. By embracing open-source technologies, companies can tap into a vast pool of talent, benefit from continuous innovation, and contribute back to the community. It's about creating a win-win situation where everyone benefits. My advice to organizations is to start small, experiment with open-source tools, and gradually expand their open-source footprint."

Interview with Lisa Garcia, Open-Source Contributor:

Lisa Garcia is an active open-source contributor who has made significant contributions to various Linux-based projects. In the interview, she shares her motivation for getting involved in open-source, discusses the challenges she encountered along the way, and offers guidance for newcomers in the open-source community. Lisa highlights the importance of documentation, communication, and perseverance in contributing to open-source projects.

Excerpt: "Getting started with open-source can be intimidating, but it's important to remember that everyone starts somewhere. My advice to newcomers is to start by identifying projects that align with your interests and skills. Read the documentation, join mailing lists or forums, and engage with the community. Don't hesitate to ask questions and seek guidance. Open-source is all about collaboration and learning from each other. With dedication and persistence, you can make meaningful contributions and become an integral part of the open-source ecosystem."

These interviews provide valuable insights and inspiration for both aspiring and experienced Linux developers and open-source contributors. They emphasize the collaborative nature of the open-source community, the impact of individual contributions, and the transformative power of Linux in shaping the future of technology.

14.3 Demonstrating industry best practices and lessons learned

In this section, we explore real-world case studies that showcase industry best practices and lessons learned when working with Linux and open-source tools. These case studies highlight successful implementations, innovative approaches, and valuable insights gained from practical experiences. Let's delve into a few examples:

Case Study: XYZ Company's Migration to Linux-Based Infrastructure

XYZ Company, a multinational organization, successfully migrated its infrastructure from proprietary systems to Linux-based solutions. This case study outlines the challenges faced, the decision-making process, and the benefits achieved through the migration. It covers topics such as cost savings, increased flexibility, improved performance, and scalability. Key lessons learned include proper planning, thorough testing, and leveraging the vibrant Linux community for support and guidance.

Case Study: Healthcare Institution's Open-Source Electronic Medical Records System

A healthcare institution implemented an open-source electronic medical records (EMR) system to streamline patient data management. This case study explores the institution's journey in adopting the EMR system, including the selection process, customization, and integration with existing infrastructure. It highlights the importance of security, data privacy, and regulatory compliance in the healthcare industry. Lessons learned encompass the significance of robust documentation, active community engagement, and continuous monitoring and updates for maintaining a secure and efficient EMR system.

Case Study: Startup's Agile Development with Linux and DevOps Practices

A startup company embraced agile development methodologies, Linux-based infrastructure, and DevOps practices to accelerate product development and deployment. This case study examines the company's transition from traditional development approaches to an agile and DevOps-centric environment. It explores the implementation of continuous integration and continuous delivery (CI/CD) pipelines, automation of deployment processes, and the utilization of cloud services. Lessons learned encompass the importance of collaboration, scalability, and the value of infrastructure-as-code in enabling rapid development and deployment cycles.

These case studies provide valuable insights into real-world scenarios where Linux and open-source tools have been effectively utilized to achieve specific objectives. They highlight the importance of proper planning, community support, security considerations, and adherence to best practices. By understanding these case studies, readers can gain inspiration and practical knowledge to apply industry best practices in their own projects.

Remember, each case study is unique, and the lessons learned may vary based on the specific requirements and challenges faced. However, studying successful implementations and lessons learned from different industries can provide valuable guidance for leveraging Linux and open-source tools effectively in various contexts.

Chapter 15: Conclusion and Future Trends

In this final chapter, we conclude our journey through Linux for Developers and reflect on the knowledge and skills you have acquired. We summarize the key takeaways and highlight the transformative power of Linux and open-source tools in the world of software development.

We emphasize the importance of continuous learning and encourage you to explore further avenues within the Linux ecosystem. The Linux community is vibrant and constantly evolving, with new technologies, frameworks, and tools emerging regularly. We urge you to stay curious, experiment with new concepts, and stay updated with the latest developments in the Linux and open-source world.

We also discuss future trends and directions that are shaping the landscape of Linux for developers. We explore topics such as containerization, cloud-native development, artificial intelligence and machine learning, edge computing, and the Internet of Things (IoT). You will gain insights into these emerging trends and their potential impact on the future of Linux development.

Lastly, we express our gratitude for joining us on this Linux journey. We hope that this book has equipped you with the knowledge, skills, and confidence to harness the potential of Linux and open-source tools in your development endeavors. Remember that Linux is more than just an operating system—it is a community-driven ecosystem that fosters collaboration, innovation, and limitless possibilities.

As you embark on your future projects, we encourage you to embrace the open-source ethos, contribute to the community, and share your knowledge and experiences with others. By doing so, you can help shape the future of Linux and inspire the next generation of developers.

15.1 Recap of key concepts and tools covered in the book

In this final chapter, we recap the key concepts and tools covered throughout the book, providing a comprehensive summary of the essential knowledge gained. Let's review some of the key concepts and tools explored in the previous chapters:

Introduction to Linux and Open Source:

- Evolution and history of Linux
- Philosophy behind open-source software
- Major Linux distributions and their characteristics

Getting Started with Linux:

- Choosing the right Linux distribution for your needs
- Installation methods: dual-boot, virtual machines, or live USB
- Basic command-line operations: navigating, file and directory management

Shell Scripting and Automation:

- Introduction to different shells (Bash, Zsh, etc.)
- Variables, conditionals, and loops in shell scripting
- Writing scripts for automating repetitive tasks

Package Management:

- Introduction to package managers: APT, YUM, and others
- Managing software repositories
- Installing, updating, and removing packages

Version Control with Git:

- Understanding Git's distributed version control system
- Setting up Git: configuration and global settings
- Basic Git operations: cloning, committing, branching, merging

Developing with Linux Tools:

- Overview of popular IDEs: Eclipse, Visual Studio Code, etc.
- Command-line text editors: Vim, Emacs, Nano
- Debugging tools: GDB, Valgrind, strace

Web Development with Linux:

- Installing and configuring Apache or Nginx web servers
- Database management with MySQL/MariaDB and PostgreSQL
- PHP, Python, or Node.js development environments

Containerization with Docker:

- Introduction to containers and containerization
- Installing Docker and managing Docker images
- Creating, running, and deploying containers with Docker

Linux Networking:

- Networking fundamentals: IP addresses, DNS, and routing
- Network configuration files and utilities
- Firewall setup with iptables or firewalld

System Administration and Security:

- User and group management: creating, modifying, and deleting accounts
- File permissions and ownership
- Securing Linux systems: firewall rules, SSH hardening, and system updates

Linux in the Cloud:

- Overview of major cloud computing platforms: AWS, Azure, GCP
- Deploying applications using cloud servers and containers
- Infrastructure as code using tools like Terraform or Ansible

Contributing to Open-Source Projects:

- Finding and evaluating open-source projects to contribute to
- Collaborating with Git: branching, merging, and resolving conflicts
- Submitting patches and pull requests

Advanced Topics and Beyond:

- Understanding the Linux kernel and its modules
- Performance tuning: optimizing system resources and processes

- High availability and clustering solutions like Pacemaker and Corosync

Case Studies and Real-World Examples:

- Showcasing successful projects using Linux in various domains
- Interviews with experienced Linux developers or open-source contributors
- Demonstrating industry best practices and lessons learned

Conclusion and Future Trends:

- Recap of key concepts and tools covered in the book

This book has provided a comprehensive exploration of Linux for developers, unlocking the potential of open-source tools. By understanding these key concepts and mastering the associated tools, you have gained the knowledge and skills to leverage Linux effectively in your development workflow. As technology continues to evolve, it is essential to stay updated with emerging trends and new tools in the Linux and open-source ecosystem. Embrace the open-source philosophy, engage with the vibrant community, and continue to enhance your proficiency in Linux and open-source technologies.

Remember, Linux offers endless possibilities, and with continuous learning and exploration, you can unlock new opportunities and contribute to the ever-growing world of open-source software.

15.2 Emerging trends in the Linux ecosystem: containers, serverless, etc.

As the Linux ecosystem continues to evolve, several emerging trends are shaping the way developers and organizations leverage the power of open-source technologies. In this section, we explore some of these trends and their potential impact on the future of Linux development.

Containerization:

Containers have revolutionized the way applications are deployed and managed. Containerization technologies like Docker provide lightweight and portable environments that encapsulate an application and its dependencies. Containers offer scalability, isolation, and consistency, making them ideal for building microservices architectures, facilitating DevOps practices, and enabling seamless application deployment across different environments.

Serverless Computing:

Serverless computing is gaining momentum as a paradigm for building and running applications without the need to manage underlying infrastructure. Platforms like AWS Lambda, Azure Functions, and Google Cloud Functions enable developers to focus solely on writing code in the form of functions, which are triggered by events and automatically scaled to handle the workload. Serverless computing offers flexibility, automatic scaling, and cost efficiency, allowing developers to build highly scalable and event-driven applications.

Edge Computing:

With the proliferation of Internet of Things (IoT) devices and the need for real-time data processing, edge computing has emerged as a powerful trend. Edge computing brings computation and data storage closer to the source of data generation, reducing latency and bandwidth requirements. Linux plays a crucial role in enabling edge computing, providing lightweight and flexible operating systems for edge devices and gateways.

Artificial Intelligence and Machine Learning:

Linux has become the platform of choice for developing artificial intelligence (AI) and machine learning (ML) applications. Frameworks like TensorFlow, PyTorch, and scikit-learn, widely used in

AI/ML development, have strong support for Linux. Linux's stability, scalability, and compatibility with powerful hardware architectures make it an ideal environment for training and deploying complex AI models.

Security and Privacy:

As cybersecurity threats continue to evolve, Linux remains a robust and secure platform for building secure systems. The Linux community actively contributes to enhancing security features, patching vulnerabilities, and implementing robust security mechanisms. Privacy concerns have also gained significant attention, leading to the development of privacy-focused Linux distributions and tools that prioritize user data protection.

Cloud-Native Development:

Cloud-native development refers to the practice of designing and building applications specifically for cloud environments. Linux, with its flexibility, scalability, and support for containerization, plays a central role in cloud-native development. Technologies like Kubernetes for orchestration and Istio for service mesh have gained popularity for managing cloud-native applications.

DevOps and Continuous Delivery:

The adoption of DevOps practices and continuous delivery has transformed software development and deployment processes. Linux, with its command-line tools, automation capabilities, and integration with popular DevOps tools like Jenkins and Git, enables seamless integration, testing, and deployment pipelines. Linux's compatibility with various CI/CD tools and infrastructure-as-code practices helps accelerate development cycles and improve collaboration between development and operations teams.

Open-Source Collaboration:

Open-source collaboration continues to be a driving force behind the Linux ecosystem. Developers and organizations are increasingly embracing open-source principles, contributing to projects, and leveraging the collective knowledge and resources of the community. The collaborative nature of Linux fosters innovation, knowledge sharing, and the development of robust and reliable software solutions.

As these trends continue to evolve, Linux remains at the forefront of enabling innovation, scalability, and flexibility in software development. By staying informed, embracing emerging technologies, and actively participating in the open-source community, developers can leverage these trends to unlock new possibilities and drive the future of Linux-based applications and systems.

15.3 Additional resources for further learning and exploration

Congratulations on completing the book "Linux for Developers: Unlocking the Potential of Open-Source Tools." As you continue your journey in Linux and open-source development, here are some additional resources to deepen your knowledge and explore new areas:

Online Documentation and Tutorials:

- **Linux Documentation Project** (www.tldp.org): A comprehensive resource with guides, how-tos, and FAQs covering various aspects of Linux.
- **Linux man pages**: Accessible through the command line, these pages provide detailed information about Linux commands and their options.

Online Learning Platforms:

- **Udemy** (www.udemy.com): Offers a wide range of Linux courses, including beginner-level introductions, advanced system administration, shell scripting, and more.

- **Coursera** (www.coursera.org): Provides online courses on Linux and related technologies from reputed universities and institutions.
- **Linux Academy** (www.linuxacademy.com): Offers in-depth Linux training courses, hands-on labs, and certification preparation.

Linux Communities and Forums:

LinuxQuestions.org (www.linuxquestions.org): A community-driven forum where you can ask questions, seek guidance, and participate in discussions related to Linux.

Reddit Linux Community (www.reddit.com/r/linux): A subreddit dedicated to discussions about Linux, news, tutorials, and sharing of resources.

Books:

- "**The Linux Command Line**" by William E. Shotts: A comprehensive guide to the Linux command line and shell scripting.
- "**Linux Pocket Guide**" by Daniel J. Barrett: A concise reference book that covers essential Linux commands, file systems, and networking.
- "**Linux Kernel Development**" by Robert Love: Provides an in-depth understanding of the Linux kernel architecture and development process.

Linux Distributions:

Ubuntu (www.ubuntu.com)
Fedora (getfedora.org)
Debian (www.debian.org)
Arch Linux (www.archlinux.org)

Open-Source Projects and Repositories:

- **GitHub** (github.com): Explore open-source projects, contribute, and learn from existing codebases.
- **GitLab** (gitlab.com): A platform for hosting and collaborating on Git repositories, including open-source projects.

Linux Conferences and Events:

Linux Foundation Events (events.linuxfoundation.org): Attend conferences, workshops, and meetups to network with experts, learn about new technologies, and stay updated with the latest trends in the Linux ecosystem.

Linux Podcasts and YouTube Channels:

- The Linux Action Show
- Linux Unplugged
- The Lunduke Show
- LearnLinuxTV (YouTube channel)

- The Linux Experiment (YouTube channel)

Remember, the Linux and open-source ecosystem is vast, dynamic, and continuously evolving. By exploring these resources and actively engaging with the community, you can expand your knowledge, stay up to date with emerging technologies, and further enhance your skills as a Linux developer.

Happy learning and happy coding!

In "Linux for Developers: Unlocking the Potential of Open-Source Tools," we embarked on a comprehensive exploration of Linux and its open-source tools, empowering developers to harness the full potential of this powerful operating system. From the foundational concepts to advanced topics, we covered a wide range of essential skills and knowledge.

We began by introducing the history and philosophy of Linux and open-source software, setting the stage for our journey. We then guided readers through the process of getting started with Linux, from choosing the right distribution to mastering basic command-line operations.

Shell scripting and automation played a crucial role in streamlining repetitive tasks, and we provided in-depth explanations and practical examples to help readers become proficient in this important skill set. We also explored package management systems, enabling developers to efficiently manage software installations, updates, and dependencies.

Version control with Git became a fundamental tool in modern software development, and we provided a comprehensive guide to its key concepts and workflows. With this knowledge, readers gained the ability to collaborate effectively and track changes in their projects.

Developing with Linux tools opened up a world of possibilities, as we explored integrated development environments (IDEs), command-line text editors, and debugging tools. This knowledge empowered developers to enhance their productivity and create high-quality code.

In the realm of web development, we guided readers through the setup and configuration of web servers, databases, and programming environments, equipping them with the skills needed to create dynamic and secure web applications.

Containerization with Docker emerged as a game-changer, and we delved into the ins and outs of this technology, allowing readers to package and deploy applications with ease across various environments.

Networking, system administration, and security formed critical pillars of a developer's skill set. We covered essential networking concepts, user and group management, file permissions, and security best practices, ensuring readers could confidently navigate these areas.

The integration of Linux with cloud computing platforms enabled developers to leverage the scalability and flexibility of the cloud. We explored deploying applications and infrastructure in the cloud, embracing infrastructure as code, and staying ahead of emerging trends.

Contributing to open-source projects became an exciting opportunity, and we provided guidance on finding projects, collaborating with Git, and making valuable contributions to the community.

Throughout the book, real-world case studies and interviews showcased successful Linux projects and provided insights into industry best practices. These practical examples reinforced concepts and inspired readers to apply their newfound knowledge.

In conclusion, "Linux for Developers: Unlocking the Potential of Open-Source Tools" has equipped developers with a solid foundation in Linux and its open-source tools. By unlocking the potential of Linux, readers can harness the power of open-source software to create innovative solutions, optimize workflows, and propel their development careers forward.

With the comprehensive knowledge gained from this book, readers can confidently navigate the ever-expanding Linux ecosystem, adapting to new technologies and embracing the boundless opportunities that lie ahead.